TEACH US TO NUMBER OUR
DAYS

WANDA MOULTRIE

WESTBOW
PRESS®
A DIVISION OF THOMAS NELSON
& ZONDERVAN

Scripture taken from the Amplified Bible, Copyright © 1954, 1958, 1962,
1964, 1965, 1987 by The Lockman Foundation. Used with permission

WestBow Press books may be ordered through booksellers or by contacting:

WestBow Press
A Division of Thomas Nelson & Zondervan
1663 Liberty Drive
Bloomington, IN 47403
www.westbowpress.com
1 (866) 928-1240

ISBN: 978-1-5127-6894-7 (sc)

Print information available on the last page.

WestBow Press rev. date: 12/28/2016

HOLD FAST

Since December 2, 2012, my walk of faith with CHRIST has been a grueling one. You may think to yourself, we all have our struggles that require faith.

As I heard the words from the Doctor at Albert Einstein Hospital in Philadelphia, Pa. (say to me as I asked questions), he's not breathing on his own, his heart is not beating on it's own, we had to remove his skull and operate on his brain, he is in a coma....and he may not make it through the night.

As my brain processed the words, as my eyes took in my son's appearance and his location, the love and pain in his fathers eyes, his siblings and Ronda Washington waiting in a room down the hall to see him. The baby boy that we were blessed to care for 26 years prior, the one who had an undying love for his family and shared my sense of humor. The child that carried his fathers name. There was a hurricane of thoughts going thru my mind and then I heard the words being said to my husband, "would you like a sedative for her?" Her? That's my son, why are they saying her? They were referring to me...CRASH AND BURN!!!

My faith was blown to smithereens! I was empty. My husband had to place me in a chair and console me. Once I could hear again, I heard Bill praying fervently for Billy and myself. Time stood still. As Bill left the room to get the others, I stood at the foot of Billy's bed and prayed. God spoke to me, reminding me that He was and still is in control and that He'd ordained this "situation". He reminded me that He would heal Billy and that I could trust Him. I had to make a decision to trust Him or myself and others. The same decision that I have to make each day as I see Billy and speak to those involved in his rehab.

Pretty soon the others were in the room and tears and emotions were flowing again. Ronda began to share her testimony of her accident at the age of 14 when the doctors told her mother that she'd never walk again, if she were to live. Pretty soon, Pastor Nate and Sis. Roz were there. I cried for Billy, I cried for myself, I cried for Bill, I cried for his siblings...I cried.

About a month later, I was at a discount store and heard the Lord say to me, Billy will drive again. Billy at this point had a Traumatic Brain Injury, could not walk, talk or do any of the things that he did previously. Seeing him in ICU in a coma w/drainage tubes attached to his brain and now in a bed with a zippered cage and a helmet on his head because he had no skull to protect his brain was real. He was a 6' 4' baby so to speak. Thank you Lord was my answer but I thought it odd for God to "out of the blue", say these words to me now. As I walked around the aisle, I saw Batman car mats sort of like the ones that Billy previously owned. I purchased them with a smile in my heart for the Lord reassuring me of His promise of healing my son.

Since that day there has been many waters trying to drown out my love for my Savior, but God has prevailed! I have cried, Lord I don't like water, Bill was the lifeguard not me and God has replied (in the words of Tony Evans), I'm not trying to drown you, just cleanse you. In the Words of Jesus, your feet are dirty.

Almost 2 1/2 years later, with many, tears, fears and prayers, this Spring, Billy will be learning to drive with an adaptive knob on the steering wheel. Like running the half marathon the course and the pains of enduring has worn on me, but through all of this, I have received a "Fresh Wind" from the Master! I have come to know and trust Him in a different light.

James says, a man may say that He has faith, but faith without works is dead, show me your faith without your works and I'll show you my faith by my works (James 2:18).

Just like Uncle Pete, there have been times where during all of this that I have taken my eyes off of Jesus, but He has been faithful. In early 2013, as Sunday Service started I would receive a note from Sis. Val which read, "Believing God with you"...this went on for months. In the following months ahead, my cell was flooded with daily text messages and prayers left on voicemail. My husband would pray over me as I slept. I know this because I know him. Many prayers that I am unaware of has gotten us to this point. God promises, He is not unfaithful to forget your work and labor of love.

I have a new understanding for being fearfully and wonderfully made, as I watch God put Humpty Dumpty back together again.

So let us seize and hold fast and retain without wavering

the hope we cherish and confess and our acknowledgement of it, for He Who promised is reliable (sure) and faithful to His word (HEBREWS 10:23)....and God does nothing "out of the blue".

TRAINING CAMP

Previously, I'd spoken about lifting weights. One of many reasons that some don't see any change when lifting weights is due to very poor training skills.

One cannot just work upper body today and lower body tomorrow with a few cardio sessions throughout the week. It has to be a daily commitment of eating right, drinking right, executing the exercise right with the right amount of reps and rest in between and then giving the body the proper amount of rest or sleep.

I usually get the question, how do I flatten my stomach or I want my arms not to jiggle when I wave bye bye to someone. The answer is to train your body. This is what Paul was telling Timothy in 1 Timothy 4:7.

I remember within the last 10 yrs, when I started hearing, " if God brings you to it, He'll bring you through it". In my mind I cringed, and thought, O no, not another one. Back when I was first saved the popular saying was, if you take one step, God will take two.

We fool ourselves by throwing the name God into the

saying and call ourselves spiritual and growing because it's on the lips of the majority. God doesn't work in majority, He always works with the remnant.

What we think in our heads, we say out of our mouths and what we say out of our mouths, we live by. All year long, the majority eat and drink how and what they desire and come the week before Mother's Day, Father's Day, Birthday or visiting another church day. The Ab Roller comes out of the closet, the Dumbbells receive some caressing and the workout gear gets worn to the mall. Come September, the treadmill becomes an indoor clothesline, the weights are again covered in dust, like some bibles and the Ab Roller becomes a lounge chair in which to sit and watch tv. Now this is all fine if you are training for the Couch Potato 2015 or the I'm not Called to that Ministry (Ever).

Paul says to "train yourselves". Strip off all of the old and new sayings so that you can see where you really are. I continue to hear that the Israelites had to make brick without straw. The scriptures never said that, rather it says that they had to get their own straw and keep the same quota. Previously all materials were supplied by the Egyptians.

If we only, preach or teach, amen or quote, we are not training ourselves to be Godly.

Coming to bible study is only a part of training, just like eating right is only a part of training. Believe it or not, I have seen overweight vegetarians. Why, because eating the good stuff is only part of training.

I Hate Math

One and one is two...two and two is four...three and three is six, echoed our second grade class as Ms. Farrell, with wooden pointer in hand (complete with rubber tip), pointed out numbers on the board. I loved math, addition was fun and I breezed right through multiplications. By the time I'd reached fifth grade, I even voluntarily attended after school tutoring to stay ahead of the game, fractions were so fun. Somewhere along the line, in Junior High I believe, I realized that the Lord had given Satan permission to add letters to numbers and that changed everything about math for me. To include letters to find the sum of...no thank you.

Much later in life, I found that God loves math as much as I used to, if not more. In 2 Peter 1 God multiplies His grace and peace unto us....here, listen to what He says,

May grace (God's favor) and peace (which is perfect well-being, all necessary good, all spiritual prosperity, and freedom from fears and agitating passions and moral conflicts) be multiplied to you in [the full, personal, precise, and correct] knowledge of God and of Jesus our Lord.

Anyone that has been in this race for sometime understands the importance of grace and peace. Grace, as I like to call it is the "grit" to run this race! Peace, that would be the mellow focus of rest during the storm. Who wouldn't want that multiplied. God has given us ev-e-rything to live this life, smothered it with promises, excuse me exceedingly great and precious promises.

He tells us to add to our faith virtue. Sometimes Bill ask me, are you ok you look kind of lethargic...I'm in need of virtue. Once I muster up my energy, I need to add some intelligence and control. This is long distance running, don't use all of your energy up front, pace yourself and know the course. When you come to a hill, don't stop, don't turn back saying, I don't do hills...press on. If you pass some one in running encourage them or better yet, don't pass, stop and pray with them, walk with them, help them carry their "weight".

Once we persevere through the math lesson we will be "equipped" for this race.

2 Peter 1:2-8

May grace (God's favor) and peace (which is perfect well-being, all necessary good, all spiritual prosperity, and freedom from fears and agitating passions and moral conflicts) be multiplied to you in [the full, personal,precise, and correct] knowledge of God and of Jesus our Lord.

For His divine power has bestowed upon us all things that [are requisite and suited] to life and godliness, through the [full, personal] knowledge of Him Who called us by and to His own glory and excellence (virtue).

By means of these He has bestowed on us His precious and exceedingly great promises, so that through them you may escape [by flight] from the moral decay (rottenness and corruption) that is in the world because of covetousness (lust and greed), and become sharers (partakers) of the divine nature.

For this very reason, adding your diligence [to the divine promises], employ every effort in exercising your faith to develop virtue (excellence, resolution, Christian energy), and in [exercising] virtue [develop] knowledge (intelligence),

And in [exercising] knowledge [develop] self-control, and in [exercising] self-control [develop] steadfastness (patience, endurance), and in [exercising] steadfastness [develop] godliness (piety),

And in [exercising] godliness [develop] brotherly affection, and in [exercising] brotherly affection [develop] Christian love.

For as these qualities are yours and increasingly abound in you, they will keep [you] from being idle or unfruitful unto the [full personal] knowledge of our Lord Jesus Christ (the Messiah, the Anointed One).

ENCOURAGED

When I had the last biopsy, I think that it's safe to say that the procedure was much more invasive than we both thought. But God has shown Himself faithful...Again!!!

The days following the operation, I tried to return to normal, but now I know that the Lord wanted me not to return to normal but to turn to Him.

As I lay in bed one day, I don't know whether or not you physically did or if you did it from afar, but the Lord told me that you were outside of the bedroom door and you prayed away the death angel and for that I am grateful. That you would have a relationship first of all with the Lord that allows you to go to Him on my behalf and one that would carry such a prayer of faith...for me!

When I have no appetite I feel so weak, but you are at every turn offering and bringing me food to encourage my eating. You've not only allowed, but you've given me rest.

When Billy exited his room this morning, he came straight to our room and looked me right in the face and said very strongly, "good morning." The look on his face said to me, I needed to see if you were ok for myself...the old Billy.

Billy is the only child of ours that has never had a complaint from his teachers about him being disrespectful. That is what prompted him to take breakfast to Pastor Nate. The Lord has started to heal in Billy the remembrance of respect for adults, particularly those over him.

I asked Billy, during our trips to Metro Drive whether or not he remembered when he was little that he wanted to be a preacher. He says he does and I asked if that's something that he would still like to do and he answered, maybe. Now I'm trying to jump the gun and think as to whether or not he will be traveling to Africa with us.

I along with you am looking to see the Lord continue to do GREAT and MIGHTY things...in this family! Ok, I'm about to turn into P. M. Smith on you...always remember and never forget...I LOVE YOU DEARLY. And like Sis. Jeter says, but God Loves you Best!

From A Product of His Mercy, to More Than a Conqueror

OLD SKOOL

During the 70's, there are several commercials that stick out in my mind at this point. Alka Seltzer whose aid was "Plop plop, fiz, fiz, O what a relief it is. Then there was Tums and it's slogan was Tum Ta Dum Dum Tums and this aid was followed (in their minds, the best), by Rolaids who quipped, How do you spell relief, R-O-L-A-I-D-S.

Now if I remember correctly, both Tums and Rolaids were portable, which was there claim to fame. They both came in small bottles or tubes for easy carrying, which meant that at any point of uneasiness your relief was a hands reach away, at least that was their selling point. These brands were also chewable. Now on the other hand Alka Seltzer had to be added to water and dissolved before ingesting. In tablet form it was too strong to purely put in ones mouth and consume. As a matter of fact the package contained a warning against doing so, stating that it would cause harm as opposed to the "relief" that was sought after.

The night before my first treatment, I received a detailed text from a dear friend whose cancer is 10 years in remission,

Praise God. Her number one on the list was drink water, leave it on your bed stand and sip all through the night. Her advice was added to my normal practice of every morning before consuming any foods, I would drink 20oz of warm water with fresh lemon juice and grated fresh ginger. Once at the hospital my meds were put on an IV drip and the volunteer offered me a large cup of water. After the first half hour, I was in the restroom every 20 minutes or so with my husband by my side, holding my hand and rolling my meds along side us down the hall opening and closing the door between us and waiting patiently for me to complete my task. After 6hrs on IV drip I was finally finished for the day. I was told that I did great with no side affects. Although, I'd noticed an uneasiness in my back, which did not alarm me, because I'd had a bad back for more than 30 years now, which during that time it had been re injured on occasion. Back at home I'm realizing that I can't get comfortable, so as I eat, I drink more water. Now being over 50 and receiving very little relief, I head for the bath tub with Epsom salts in tow which proved to me that the irritation was not topical but internal. In my feeble mind I lay on a heating pad which was followed by a heated hand held massager which gave about 20% more relief.

As I sat at the kitchen table with Billy laughing and talking and enjoying his company, the Holy Spirit spoke to my heart....hot water. I filled my 20oz mug with water and once heated I drop in one green and one peppermint tea bag. After about 10 minutes later I had experienced the most relief of all. I was able to laugh with my son without the cramping in my digestive system. I was able to turn to the side without apprehension of feeling pulling, pinching and tightness. I was able to lay down with my husband in comfort. All because the temperature of the water that Christ had chosen for me was Hot in order to distribute my prescribed meds and attack in my body that which was causing me to not to look, act and appear normal to the trained eye.

After about 3 hours of sleep and much needed rest, I wake up with minimal cramping but in sheer delight, but I am faced with the same question. Am I willing to be lazy and live in discomfort even though I may look normal to those around me or am I willing to get up and drink more hot water for the cleansing and healing of not mine but His body.

I leave with you Billy's favorite verses:

1 Corinthians 6:19-20

Do you not know that your body is the temple (the very sanctuary) of the Holy Spirit Who lives within you, Whom you have received [as a Gift] from God? You are not your own,

You were bought with a price [purchased with a preciousness and paid for, made His own]. So then, honor God and bring glory to Him in your body.

THE INCISION

Have you ever experienced a tooth ache? When we have these ailments, our human inclination tells us to steer clear of the aggravated area, to treat it with kindness and loving care.

We brush softly or not at all. We look at it 50 times a day to make sure that it is free of contaminates, as far as the naked eye can see. We refuse to chew on that side of the mouth. If the area is sensitive to cold, we use a straw. We eat only foods that will easily travel thru the mouth, for fear of anything adhering to the teeth.

On the other hand when we go to the dentist, he will take seemingly the sharpest of instruments and begin to probe into the affected or infected area, causing more pain than we care to be acquainted with at one time. As he begins to pick and prod, dig and push you may wonder why you are paying him to cause you so much pain, when all you wanted was relief.

I myself had wisdom teeth that were so impacted that my dentist had to cut my jaw to retrieve them and then stitch me back together. My mouth split in the outer corners and it hurt me to talk for weeks to come. My husband was shocked to find that I had nothing or so little to say.

The dentist has something that we don't have. More than his arsenal of sharp instruments and a license to look into our mouths, he has a desire to get to the root of our problem, correct it and steer you into the path of healing, which includes enough knowledge for you not to return to his presence in the same dilemma.

This to me is a picture of Psalms 139: 23-24. As Christians we mistakingly think that telling the Lord what we are willing to tell Him is allowing Him to search us. When the Lord searches us, it should be a picture of us in the dentist chair with our mouths open so wide rendering us speechless and open to the probing of "The Skilled One", to get to the heart of the matter.

In Isaiah 6:5, Isaiah acknowledges his sinful state as he stands before a Holy God. In Luke 5:8 Peter falls on his face and begs Jesus to leave his presence because of his own sinful state. And we the modern day Israelites boldly parade our sin(s) before God and declare ourselves searched and cleaned thereby being in a worse state than at the beginning.

We need to fall on our faces before the Lord that made us and allow Him to diagnose us and then take His two-edged sword and administer healing so that we are not constantly at the same impasse. Remember, God hates pride, so let's humble ourselves before the Master as He does the probing and the digging.

When was the last time, if any that you were speechless before the Lord?

CHOSEN

You are a chosen generation...a royal priesthood...a holy nation.

As a new babe in Christ, I had an abundance of favorite scriptures. The afore mentioned is just one of those. Growing up as the youngest of four children, I was as it seemed always put on the back burner of things. I was the first to go to bed and the last to know what happened and when. And when it came to games, whether Jacks, Tin Can Alley, Red Light, Double Dutch or Roller Derby, I was never chosen. Life seemed to me one heartache after another because my heart longed to be chosen.

Imagine the excitement at the age of 17 when I clearly understood that out of all of the people in the world and amid all of my transgressions that I was still chosen.

This thing called salvation is amazing, because not only was I chosen but I was chosen by thee "best." Within 2 years of my salvation, I'd met and married the man that, here we are again was "chosen" for me by the One that chose me.

I was sooo excited on that day, that had no one else shown up, I may not have noticed any way.

We started our marriage off with a beautiful 4 year old and 3 years later the Lord chose to increase the size of our quiver. The following year...God's increase again. We assumed that our family was complete, but 3 years later God chose to complete us with Douglas.

During this 10 years of marriage, I can't remember ever turning down a blessing that the Lord had chosen for the Moultrie family. We've even received day old bread when our bread box was empty.

On May 14, 2015, when the oncology doctor called with my diagnosis, I clearly understood that it was of Gods choosing. Like all the other things that He'd chosen for me, I'm sure that there will be aspects that I don't like or even agree with, but none of them should interfere with my excepting His choosing me. Proverbs 10:22 states

The blessing of the Lord—it makes [truly] rich, and He adds no sorrow with it [neither does toiling increase it].

DESTINY

For the past several weeks, ringing in my heart and ears are the line of words in a song close to my heart. Your destiny is too important to give up for anything (Destiny by Kevin Levar).

I began to ask God, what and where is my destiny? Early on in my marriage, I knew that raising a Godly seed is what God required of me. At this point in my life, I'd raised my children and am now a grandmother of six. Our oldest son, now 29, suffered a Traumatic Brain Injury (TBI), at the age of 26 from an auto accident. After having a crainectomy and brain surgery and not expected to live through the night, six months later he was sent home to be cared for. Having quit my jobs to become his full time caregiver was appointed to me by the Lord.

Not having any expertise in this field, much like the beginning stages of my marriage, I again set out to please the Lord, becoming my Son's therapist, nurse, nutritionists, social worker, chauffeur, and whatever he needed me to be. There where so many missing pieces in his life. Like an old cassette tape or computer, he had all of the information post accident, but many times there was no communication from his brain to his body, which left him with cognitive as well as physical disabilities. I hadn't realized it then, but now I see that I was trying to be his "binding agent." Casting my needs and myself aside, I jumped in with all that I had of me and became whatever he needed. Due to his TBI, his brain would not show him things that were right in front of his face, but there was no need to fear because "Christian Mom" was here.

Able to do 10 loads of laundry a day, which included wash, dry and put away. Had the ability to make appointments over the phone while planning and cooking a nutritious meal. Having devotions twice daily while incorporating speech therapy. Not missing a church service while still having a smile on my face and a praise in my heart. Look, up in the sky, it's a bird, it's a plane...it's Christian Mom!"

About 2 years out from my son's accident, the Lord alerted me to things that were a little off with me. As I stood on a chair to put up some Christmas decorations, I became a little dizzy. Within a week a had the same feeling while standing at the top of the stairs. I knew that I needed to have it checked but once the thought of caregiver entered my head I soon forgot. Within the next month or so there were other little " differences" that I noticed. During the waiting period, the arthritis in my knee caused it to swell and I could no longer do my morning run on the treadmill which followed my devotions. The pain was so intense that I could no longer bend or place pressure of any kind on that knee.

As I limped around the house but mostly lay with my leg elevated and wrapped in a heating pad...it was there that the Lord spoke to my heart and told me of my condition. At each turn during the coming months, I heard clearly what God was saying to me. Each time I thought, did I hear Him right, He would reassure me that I heard Him correctly. At the time I had no tears, no fear only certainty of what was said to me. I was now living in the realization that the Lord was teaching me to live "day by day."

Appointment day was finally here, a two week waiting period.

The dictionary describes destiny as the power or agency that determines the course of events.

Psalms 86:1

Bow down: stretch out; to bend down

Poor: afflicted, weak, humble, lowly

Needy: in need; chiefly poor, subject to oppression and abuse. In the sense of want (especially in feeling)

Vs. 5

Call: cry out; cry (for help), call (with name of God)

Mark 4:39

Peace: to be silent, involuntary stillness, or an inability to speak

Still: to close the mouth with a muzzle

As long as I don't look like Bill Johnson when this is all said and done

If it proves to be a sickness unto death than it proves that I still run faster than you

The gift, it looks good on me.

YESTERDAY

On yesterday, as I started my day, I had this peculiar feeling that followed me for most of the day. It was the feeling of "where am I?" As my day progressed it became my prayer for the day. As I changed beds, dusted and vacuumed floors, washed, dried, folded and put away laundry, prepared meals for Billy and ran a few errands, my prayer changed from Lord where am I to "do I really need to know where I am Lord or should I be satisfied with the fact that you know where I am?"

The bizarre thing is, the prayer of where am I seemed to be a continuous prayer whereas the latter prayer brought "peace and calm" to my heart and mind. The thoughts of the Psalmist began to flood my mind, Where could I go from Your Spirit? Or where could I flee from Your presence? (Psalms 139:7).

My thoughts became clearer, my energy level took an upswing. The pains in my body that I'd been experiencing seemed to carry me as opposed to hindering me from my daily task. At the point that I would normally call it quits and put my feet up I continued on.

Do you think that Christ experienced the same in Hebrews 12:2, Who for the joy that was set before Him. Once the Holy Spirit was able to get me to take my eyes off of me and my pain and the diagnostic test that I was to have in 4 days and the house work and the appointments and the meals and my sons' care and my other 3 children and my husband who was fasting for me today and his needs and my needs, our grandchildren and seemingly a thousand other things...I found rest or rather it, He found me. In the midst of it all, even when I did not realize that a storm was brewing, but the Savior, the One in whose presence I can never leave, the One who holds me by His hand. The One in Whom the darkness can hide nothing from. The Master Weaver that knit me together in my mothers womb, said to me, "Peace be still...and know that I am God".

The Race, The Rest

On last night I was able to attend my Breast Cancer Awareness Class for the first time. Outside of myself, there were 8 ladies, with 1 of them being a nutritionist and 1 other being a life coach, but all having had or currently having cancer.

There was a lady present who during her treatments and operations, had only her dog to assist her. Then there was another from Germany, who when she told her children of her diagnosis, they replied to her, "breast cancer is expected at your age, you'll be fine." We also have a women younger than myself whose struggle has been to endure operations during this season of her only child (son) preparing for graduation from elementary school.

Then we have myself, who since May, have been made to put my feet up, take naps, cease driving, cooking and cleaning. I've been told don't think about it, tell me what you want, do you need anything, you're doing too much, Momi I'll take you, do you have an appointment today, go help Grammy, I have it, you ok with food, what does your family like to eat. If I get up at 6am, I have text messages that arrived at 5, I've received songs, prayers, emails, cards, flowers, visits, and hugs. I've been given Reverse Osmosis Water. Douglas always comes home with, everybody asked for you and this person asked for your phone number. Billy is up at 1am, slicing oranges for me so that I will not have to prepare my own breakfast, and then he serves them to me on that morning. He has been striving to do so many things that he lost as a result of his Brain Injury. I was told that 7-14 days after my 1st treatment I'd loose my hair, the hair that I'd spent the last 2 years growing out, I had visions of waking up to clumps of matted hair in bed. The Lord sent me a Barber that made it so painless to get my buzz cut, that I had forgotten that I was in his chair. If I were to add my hubby, Mr. Incredible to this list, it would consume your entire day. But believe you, he is just that...Mr. Incredible.

All present at the class agreed on one thing and that is that I will be fine because I have such great support and a few even stated that they envied me.

This all brings to mind for me 1 Corinthians 9:24

Do you not know that in a race all the runners compete, but [only] one receives the prize? So run [your race] that you may lay hold [of the prize] and make it yours. Many of you have told me for years that you don't like running, but from where I sit, literally sit, you are running well and I would like to encourage you to run on! I am so blessed that in your running, it is allowing me to rest. I am super thankful that Jesus who cannot lie has promised not to be unrighteous and forget your work and labor of love that you have shown (Heb. 6:10).

For those of you that can, give yourselves a pat on that

back and those that can't, pat the back in front of you...you deserve it. Your running has allowed me to rest and for that I am grateful.

http://youtu.be/zt67dqnWDHw

THE VIRUS

Feelings are catchy. Have you ever attended a wedding or funeral and cried because someone else was crying or laughed because someone else did? Well you caught an emotional virus.

There is a 90's movie by the name of "Con Air" starring Nicholas Cage. Cage played an inmate by the name of Poe, who was being transported on a plane with other inmates, one whom was named Cyrus the Virus. That name sticks in my head. I've often wondered how he came about obtaining that name. Did he have an infectious personality? Did he have some sort of illness that he transferred to others? Was he so persuasive in his evil ways that he attached his ways to others and they in turn became like him?

Christ calls us to be wise as serpents, but harmless as doves (Matt. 10:16). He would also have us to be well, whole, healthy. But I believe that he wants us to be like Cyrus the Virus. He wants us to be infectious with what He has given us...what He has done for us, what He has placed in us.

To catch a virus, it has to be transferred through some type of bodily fluid. It can be picked up in the air from the secretions of a cough or sneeze from someone within your comfort zone. Do you get the picture? In order to infect or affect someone you have to be in close proximity. One on one, face to face. No social media, and no text messaging.

Jesus said to Let your lights shine before, in front of, in the presence of, near men.

Paul earnestly prayed for the Lord to save others and as a result of his prayers he himself was landed in prison and instead of complaining, he became a virus. Acts 28:23-24 states, So when they had set a day with him, they came in large numbers to his lodging. And he fully set forth and explained the matter to them from morning until night, testifying to the kingdom of God and trying to persuade them concerning Jesus both from the Law of Moses and from the Prophets.

And some were convinced and believed what he said, and others did not believe. Verse 30 tells us that for the space of 2 yrs, in prison he infected people.

If those in our presence are acting ungodly, they have either been infected by us or need to be affected by us.

Heart Murmur

During my last pregnancy, in my second trimester, my doctor told me a few things about me that no doctor before him had. The first he said is that I have scoliosis which is a curvature of my spine. He stated that it was slight but noticeable enough for me to draw disability. Well being under 30 years of age, and enjoying running, exercise and all of the freedoms that the Lord had afforded me, since it was not bothering me, than I refused to bother it.

The other thing that he found was a heart murmur. Now this caught my attention for a moment. I questioned my doctor and when he reassured me that it would not interfere with my pregnancy, labor and delivery, I placed it on the back burner and continued to move ahead. If I remember correctly, I didn't even share this information with my hubby right away, because to me it was just not that important.

Scoliosis can cause back, abdominal and chest pain due to the curving of the spine. These pains will affect the way that the sufferer will sit, walk and stand. The diagnosis encouraged me to exercise more in order to strengthen the muscles to support my back, thereby lessening the effects of a weak back.

As for a heart murmur the side effects can range from shortness of breath, dizziness,and palpitations, to congestion of the lungs. Personally, it's the heart palpitations for me.

Even before our marriage, I distinctly remember Min. Bill doing a lesson on the theme of the book of Ephesians, sit, walk and stand. Christ has raised us up to sit together, we are to walk worthy of the vocation in which He called us and after the storms of life have beat vehemently upon us, having done all we are to stand.

I can pinpoint specific times when my husband said to me, don't do that and my heart murmured, what difference does it make or I know what I'm doing. I have been in conversation with the unsaved and heard the Holy Spirit say to me, mention the Father and the Son, and my next comment was, Ok, it was good to see you, and then I murmured they had to go anyway. The Spirit has told me to turn the TV off and open my bible and I've murmured, but this is sooo funny.

What is it in your life that causes you great pain and deters you not to sit, walk and stand? Or does your heart murmur make you stop every few yards when running for Jesus?

Hebrews 12:12-13 So then, brace up and reinvigorate and set right your slackened and weakened and drooping hands and strengthen your feeble and palsied and tottering knees,

And cut through and make firm and plain and smooth, straight paths for your feet [yes, make them safe and upright and happy paths that go in the right direction], so that the lame and halting [limbs] may not be put out of joint, but rather may be cured.

Jude 1:14-16

It was of these people, moreover, that Enoch in the seventh [generation] from Adam prophesied when he said, Behold, the Lord comes with His myriads of holy ones (ten thousands of His saints)

To execute judgment upon all and to convict all the impious (unholy ones) of all their ungodly deeds which they have committed [in such an] ungodly [way], and of all the severe (abusive, jarring) things which ungodly sinners have spoken against Him.

These are inveterate murmurers (grumblers) who complain [of their lot in life], going after their own desires [controlled by their passions]; their talk is boastful and arrogant, [and they claim to] admire men's persons and pay people flattering compliments to gain advantage.

THE VOICE

In this past week while in a different room, I have confused Leslie's voice and footsteps with those of Solana's. We always have a laugh about it because after I've done it a couple of times Leslie knows that I know longer care because I just want what I want at the time of confusion.

When Billy was in his mid teens and he'd arrive home from school, he would slow his footsteps as he approached me and as he got closer but just before I could lay my eyes on him he would say something like, "Hey Babe" or "Babe, what's for dinner?" Now the first time that he pulled this trick, it was so hilarious for him and I. Then he'd wait about a month, when he thought that I was off guard and try it again.

With Douglas, it was always the music or the running up and down the stairs to see what foods are in the refrigerator that were not there 5 minutes ago.

Stacey, that's our math wiz that retains information that everyone else has forgotten existed...the History buff. One day when Stacey and I were in Walmart, Douglas was home with Billy. She called to see if Doug was still home and he told her that he left about maybe 45mins ago but not quite an hour, and her face twisted. I responded to her, I will smack you if you don't stop turning that conversation into a math problem and we both had a good laugh, because it was already done.

Then we have a popular TV show, one which I've never watched, called The Voice. This show focuses primarily on singing ability and prowess of the artist alone.

In Psalms 32:8 Jesus tells us, I [the Lord] will instruct you and teach you in the way you should go; I will counsel you with My eye upon you. Now because He is immutable and cannot lie, it's a true statement, but this is His part. We have a part as well. John 10:4 says to the Christian, When he has brought his own sheep outside, he walks on before them, and the sheep follow him because they know his voice.

Now with Leslie and Solana, purely on my part, I was confused as to the voice that I was hearing and even willing to give information to, even after I realized that it was not whom I needed it to be.

Billy, he was the trickster and sought out to confuse me and in the end came very close to it. Before he ceased this charade, I would have to think to myself, what, wait.

Douglas was a young teen and I would walk through the hallway headed to the office prepared to open up to my husband on the piano and find Douglas.

When in conversation with Stacey, I'm always saying to her ok Bill Moultrie and everything is not a math problem and by the way Billy even with his brain injury has recently tutored Solana in math and her teacher was so elated that it was all correct.

John 10:27 says The sheep that are My own hear and are listening to My voice; and I know them, and they follow Me.

Self explanatory right...the sheep that are His own, first check point. Point number two, am I listening to His voice? Now if I have these items covered, Christ is faithful to do His part...exceeding and abundantly.

Who am I listening to today? Is it the Master or does it just sound and walk like the the Master? Does the music that is being played sooth my soul like the Master's but proves to be a black market copy. Is the conversation being, the same as the Master's conversation, but yet and still not Him?

There are people and things that have the talent and abilities to capture our devotion and following.

John 10:5 says,They will never [on any account] follow a stranger, but will run away from him because they do not know the voice of strangers or recognize their call.

http://youtu.be/SKeTQ1ZHqgA

GEAR UP

Growing up as children, my siblings and I were never allowed to participate in sports, at least not until my older brothers' high school years where he played basketball at Dunbar Senior High.

I can remember gym class, trying to get my mother to purchase the uniform which I needed. All those my age can identify with the one piece zip or snap front ordeal that we had to endure, and when they were too small, well you remember.

I despised gym. Mainly because I was quite often unprepared. Although I was the youngest of four, having had two brothers and one sister, I received everybody's hand me downs. It was like being a Christian, no male or female, you had a need and it was supplied. And sometimes after being worn by three others, once I received the item, in many cases, it was worn out.

In gym class we sat in a huddle or on the bleachers. At role call, when you heard your name you had to step out from the crowd showing that you were ready to participate for the day. If your uniform or shoes were raggedy the teacher would loudly say so and make you sit against the wall labeling you as unprepared. Sometimes, depending on the teacher, she would call all unprepared students lastly, in their own little group, while everyone else watched and laughed as they were put on display. Further comments were made as to why the performance was not up to par, that is if you were allowed to participate.

This type of behavior took the wind out of my sails. I used to like attending school. I looked forward to learning new things and spending time with others.

Meanwhile back at home, sharing all of this with my mother, in my mind she would surely produce a much needed uniform or tennis shoes for me...after all it was a part of my grade. She usually commented that she did not have the money. This kept me for a while, until I realized that everyday she played the lottery as well as the street numbers. I began to wonder, how can she have monies for that and not me. Well this added insult to injury. That is until I reached the eighth and ninth grade and all of the afore prepared girls were too cute to put forth the much needed effort on the rings, parallel bars and the horse. The uneven parallel bars were a little tricky, doing a birds nest on the rings was fun, but I became one with the horse and the others were full with envy.

Earlier on I allowed the actions of my teachers and my mother to dull my purpose for "being." This is what happened to the Galatians. Paul asked the question, "You were running the race nobly. Who has interfered in (hindered and stopped you from) your heeding and following the Truth (Galatians 5:7)?

I'm reminded of those that attend basketball games and their sole purpose is to purchase paraphernalia and sit behind the opponents basket, waving and yelling to keep them from advancing. Paul says, " I wish those who unsettle and confuse you would [go all the way and] cut themselves off!

For you, brethren, were [indeed] called to freedom; only [do not let your] freedom be an incentive to your flesh and an opportunity or excuse [forselfishness], but through love you should serve one another.

Now back at gym class there was a large cardboard box with gym suits from previous students, left in lockers unclaimed. These items were at the disposal of the teacher. At anytime she could either give them to the student, loan them for the week, school year or day. But her flesh was gratified by receiving laughter from students concerning students in need.

Jesus says, if we are led by the Spirit than we are not under the law. Galatians 5:19-26

Now the doings (practices) of the flesh are clear (obvious): they are immorality, impurity, indecency,

Idolatry, sorcery, enmity, strife, jealousy, anger (ill temper), selfishness, divisions (dissensions), party spirit (factions, sects with peculiar opinions, heresies),

Envy, drunkenness, carousing, and the like. I warn you beforehand, just as I did previously, that those who do such things shall not inherit the kingdom of God.

But the fruit of the [Holy] Spirit [the work which His presence within accomplishes] is love, joy (gladness), peace, patience (an even temper, forbearance), kindness, goodness (benevolence), faithfulness,

Gentleness (meekness, humility), self-control (self-restraint, continence). Against such things there is no law [that can bring a charge].

And those who belong to Christ Jesus (the Messiah) have crucified the flesh (the godless human nature) with its passions and appetites and desires.

If we live by the [Holy] Spirit, let us also walk by the Spirit. [If by the Holy Spiritwe have our life in God, let us go forwardwalking in line, our conduct controlled by the Spirit.]

Let us not become vainglorious and self-conceited, competitive and challenging and provoking and irritating to one another, envying and being jealous of one another.

Time to put our armor on, looks like we have a lot of work to do.

TASTE

Before chemo, I enjoyed getting up in the morning and eating bananas while having my morning devotions. After chemo began, my taste immediately changed. Now I find myself wanting and craving certain foods. Even after I eat them the craving is not always satiated, because I can't necessarily taste what I have consumed.

When in bondage in Egypt, the Israelites cried to God for freedom. Once freed, they quickly cried to God for the leeks and the garlic and cucumbers, and the melons and the fish and onions.

It is astonishing to me how a desire, a fondness, an appetite will make us forget about the years of bondage and pain that was associated with the satisfaction of our cravings.

I've heard time and time again, what you feed grows. This is a concept that was always hard for the participants at exercise class to grasp. I constantly heard the comment, that this runs in my family or I like to do it this way. Sometimes in my mind and usually out of my mouth came the words, no it's in your family because you don't run.

It was never grasped that within us, through the power of the Holy Spirit, by Christ we can "change" things that are generational. But if we continue to satisfy that "taste" we will constantly live in defeat and gravitate toward the flesh with no victory.

Unless, unless we have tasted the good Word of God and we drift toward Him and His "goodness" on a daily basis. Now tasting of God's Word is sort of like eating during chemo. Sometimes I receive the full flavor of the foods that I eat and other times, not so much. I've known intellectually, but in these past few months, I've learned that tasting is not always about the flavour, but more so the taking in and the nourishment.

This is what was provided in the wilderness for God's people via His manna. Manna was not only sweet to eat but it provided all nourishment needed for each person willing to partake of it. I've also learned that when I eat, I need to concentrate on what it taste like now and not what it taste like before as well as the nourishment that it is providing for my body.

This can be a hard pill to swallow with God when we are not willing to partake of what He is providing...not what we want, the garlic, fish, onions, you get the picture. When we want what others have, what's available, the latest and greatest, so we thought, we loose...miserably.

Another thing that I would share at exercise class, was to be patient, exercise regularly and eat right and the change will come. Impatience always produce the purchase of weight loss gimmicks. After all if you gain 50 pounds within 12 months and Slimfast can take it off in 2 months, you should think about side effects. Quick methods with the absence of consistent work always produces a return of what you think you got rid of and that return is always with a vengeance.

Hebrews 6:4-6

For it is impossible [to restore and bring again to repentance] those who have been once for all enlightened, who have consciously tasted the heavenly gift and have become sharers of the Holy Spirit,

And have felt how good the Word of God is and the mighty powers of the age and world to come,

If they then deviate from the faith and turn away from their allegiance—[it is impossible] to bring them back to repentance, for (because, while, as long as) they nail upon the cross the Son of God afresh [as far as they are concerned] and are holding [Him] up to contempt and shame and public disgrace.

CLEAN

The dictionary defines the word clean as unsoiled, unstained, free from dirt or free from foreign or extraneous matter. Psalms 51:10 states, Create in me a clean heart, O God, and renew a right, persevering, and steadfast spirit within me.

This verse came to mind today as I thought and prayed for our dear sister Lisa, who's having a heart operation this morning. Now while I don't have all of the details, which is not important, because the Lord Who made her does. But as I prayed, Psalms 51:10 came to mind, which was followed by the thought of cleaning. Before I make a trip to the grocery store each week, I try to do a simple cleaning in my refrigerator. It makes it free from dirt and unsoiled, you know foods that were dropped, spilled and not wiped up. Depending on how detailed I am at cleaning, items that are going bad can be removed as well. Now when I don't perform a simple cleaning, than a more detailed job is needed. As it is with our hearts. When we don't allow God to create in me a clean heart on a daily basis, He has to do a more detailed cleaning.

As we pile stuff into our hearts, including the Word of God and not use it when and for what it is intended, our hearts require a cleaning. When we allow and invite things into our lives that are not of God, our hearts require a cleaning.

That being said who is willing to take Lisa's place this morning and/or allow God to Create in me a clean heart. You see cleaning means a great deal of wiping, scrubbing, cutting, removing, and replacing in order to become clean. What may be clean to me, may not be clean to you, but in this case, it's the Lords cleanliness that matters.

Psalms 51:10-17

Create in me a clean heart, O God, and renew a right, persevering, and steadfast spirit within me.

Cast me not away from Your presence and take not Your Holy Spirit from me.

Restore to me the joy of Your salvation and uphold me with a willing spirit.

Then will I teach transgressors Your ways, and sinners shall be converted and return to You.

Deliver me from bloodguiltiness and death, O God, the God of my salvation, and my tongue shall sing aloud of Your righteousness (Your rightness and Your justice).

O Lord, open my lips, and my mouth shall show forth Your praise.

For You delight not in sacrifice, or else would I give it; You find no pleasure in burnt offering.

My sacrifice [the sacrifice acceptable] to God is a broken spirit; a broken and a contrite heart [broken down with sorrow for sin and humbly and thoroughly penitent], such, O God, You will not despise.

My Sentiments

It is way too hot today. It has rained everyday for a week and a half, I wish that it would quit already. Have you ever uttered these words with hopes that God would hear and answer? Let's look at the other side of these requests.

I have a small vegetable garden in which I'd planned in April to add seeds and plants in May. Due to the fact that the Lord directs my steps, I was unable to get my seeds started and did not get my tomato plants in the ground until late June. Well by the time this was accomplished, the temperatures outside were sweltering, my energy level was at a low and my time has to be limited in the sun. I was so concerned with my plants taking root and flourishing or possibly dying, that I prayed fervently for the Lord to take care of my investment. So for about a week and a half, "the heavens declared the glories of God," and I could not have been happier. My vegetation received the proper amounts of water to allow the roots to dig deep, stand tall and produce fruit.

The heavens declare the glory of God, hmmmm. Why

is it that we only think that this verse holds true, when the sun is shinning, stars are twinkling and the moon is at an all time high? As we pray and ask God for wants and sometimes needs, whom are we considering, just self or others that will be affected? I'm sure that while I prayed for my plants and God sent the rain that there was someone with a leaky roof and or wet basement praying for the rain to stop.

At times we fail to see the forest for the trees, but God Himself declares that His ways and thoughts are not our ways and thoughts, and for that I give Him Praise. So the next time, (and believe me, it will happen), that the wind is seemingly blowing too hard, or you have a flat tire just before a job interview or the basement floods, the roof leaks or the rain in your life just seems like it will not stop. Pause and consider Jesus. Without the proper balance of sun and water, your roots cannot dig deep, you will not stand tall and as far as producing fruit, not so much. After all who wants to an evergreen tree in the middle of spring and summer when colors are in abundance?

Jeremiah 29:11-13

For I know the thoughts and plans that I have for you, says the Lord, thoughts and plans for welfare and peace and not for evil, to give you hope in your final outcome.

Then you will call upon Me, and you will come and pray to Me, and I will hear and heed you.

Then you will seek Me, inquire for, and require Me [as a vital necessity] and find Me when you search for Me with all your heart.

Romans 8:28

We are assured and know that [God being a partner in

their labor] all things work together and are [fitting into a plan] for good to and for those who love God and are called according to [His] design and purpose.

http://youtu.be/kDspAFLflew

SOMETHING ABOUT
THAT NAME

When I was blessed to obtain my CDL's and a job as a school bus driver, I often asked a question to the other drivers. The question was, "do you know such and such" and the answer was usually, what is their bus number? I quickly learned that bus drivers were known by their number more than their names.

Each time I go to the hospital to receive any type of medication, even if is given 6 times on that same day and by the same nurse, I'm asked to give my full name and birth date to see if I am who I said I am or whom the staff believe me to be.

The more that I state my name the more awkward it sounds to even me. I think, do these 3 names go well together, why were they chosen for me, would I have spelled them this way, when I was born, did my parents realize that God had a job(s) for just me, did they care, do I care, have I excepted the name given me?

The name that has been given me is not Wanda Diane

Moultrie, well it is but Christian is what I'm referring to. Proverbs 22:1 states, A GOOD name is rather to be chosen than great riches, and loving favor rather than silver and gold.

My name is my identity, my reputation, how I am known...that is Wanda D. Moultrie. Now a Good name for me is Christian. Ironically this name carries more weight than my government name. But some Christians are still not aware of this fact. It is a belief that this name carries prestige in the sense that if someone sees me coming that they should speak first, get out of their seats and kneel in my presence. Do you remember what Jesus told the disciples when He empowered them for ministry and they had exorcised demons? Don't rejoice because you have been given power over Satan, but rejoice because your names have been written in heaven (Luke 10:1-20). Because their government name was written, it has been translated into Christian.

A Christian is one who follows the life and teachings of Jesus Christ...follows not just quotes. Today a majority preaches mainly of prosperity, when Jesus' teachings carries with it suffering as well. If you look at His earthly life, suffering is a large part of it. Most of us miss it because Christ never complained and be wailed through life. He continued to trust Himself to the One that judges righteously (1Peter 2:23). We never hear Him as a lad saying things like, "why don't I have any friends, why do I have to be in the temple at the age of twelve and be about my Father's business and my parents left me and didn't know it til 2 days later.? If I'm a carpenter, can I make go carts and sell them for a profit? I'd like to buy my Mom a house on a hill, that I actually own anyway because after all, ah hmm, I am not only King but the King of Kings. In about 4,015 days, I'm scheduled to die on the cross for a bunch of ungrateful sinners that hate my guts, won't talk to me after I saved them, bicker and complain between each other, tell others that I said and told them to do things that I never authorized, don't honor Me and the Father, believe that My Spirit is a thing or a Genie in a bottle and worst of all I have to be separated for the only time in history from my Father, when all I did was loved hem...to death, and I still think that Barabbus would be a better candidate then me.

This is what the name Jesus carries as His follower, suffering before glory. What does His name mean to you?

El Shimchath Gili: The God of my Exceeding Joy Psalms 43:4

RESULTS EQUALS REST

Have you ever been invited to a formal event or asked to be a part of a wedding party that was due to take place months later? Or felt the warm April sunshine and knew that short sleeve tops were only weeks away. Usually once the excitement of the idea of the event wears off, the individual in receipt of the invite does one of two things, maybe both. A change takes place in what or how much food is consumed on a daily basis and a exercise plan is implemented.

Once the event has come and gone, pictures have been taken and placed on the mantle and on every social media known to man, the mind says rest, take thine ease. You have achieved what you worked at, no need to work any longer, just rest. Before you know it, the clothes that were worn before the invite came in the mail are too snug. You can't understand (as you look at the photos), how this happened.

In your heart, you all have an unspoken plan. In this case the plan was to be a participant, look well in the outfit, receive compliments, take pictures and possibly not spill food on ourselves. Once the plan has been executed, you rest...and become lazy. This is why you convince yourself that the polyester/rayon blend has shrunk or I had too much salt last night. Anything but the truth.

God in His infinite wisdom has decided not to show us the bulk if any of the results of our "laboring in the vineyard," knowing that we will become lazy and take our ease...before "The Work" is complete.

In our hearts and mind we may have a plan but in God's kingdom, He has The Plan. Isaiah 55:8-9 states, For My thoughts are not your thoughts, neither are your ways My ways, says the Lord.

For as the heavens are higher than the earth, so are My ways higher than your ways and My thoughts than your thoughts.

While my plan, your scheme, our ideas may be good, God's Plan is perfect. Within the past 4 years, I have seen what man, Christian man has said all is lost and once God's plan unfolded, salvation has come.

The Air I Breathe

During the 80's as I conducted exercise class, one of the things that I stressed was to breathe while performing any type of exercise. I usually received flack and laughter from the comment. Who would not know to breathe is what I was told, how long did it take you to come up with that one? Several months later a few people came back saying, I realized that I was holding my breath and I had to laugh, as I thought about you.

Once I started treatments, my strength disappeared like a thief in the night. The Grammy of 6, that had been married for 32 yrs, that previously was able to bench press 150 lbs (in my younger days), could not shower and get dressed without needing a nap or carry a basket of laundry from the basement up 2 flights of stairs without taking a nap, and consistently dropping the basket in route.

As, I lay in bed for hours and days, weeks and months, I realized that I wasn't breathing correctly. As someone that previously avoided medications of all types, and now constantly being loaded with toxins, it affected every aspect of my "being."

My daily prayers became Lord, teach me how to breath as my breathing had become more shallow which would tire me quickly and make me less than effective. Jesus, I need you to renew my strength, both spiritual and physical.

As the medications, which includes steroids started to take their effect on my life, I began to have sleepless nights and a change in appetite. Just like during Billy's "ordained" time of brokenness and healing, I could see Jesus in a different light as I sat in the dark.

It drew my mind back six years ago when Cochise died and my children bought Chariot for me, for those that don't know they are my beloved dogs. Chariot for some reason would wake up in the middle of the night in her cage and yelp loudly and consistently...every night. I would pray for her to cease this behavior, I would scold her for it, but as soon as my head hit the pillow, she would start up again. I thought that I had come up with this bright idea, but pretty soon the Holy Spirit revealed that it was the Lord and not I. The idea was whenever Chariot would wake up, God had something to say to me. I was to get up, get dressed get Chariot and go for a walk. I tried walking around the school, a 5 minute walk and heading home on the first couple of days. It proved unsuccessful as her yelping increased. So my walking increased. On one of our walks to W. Bel Air, it was humid, I was tired and Chariot was full of life at about 3:30 am. I stopped at the corner of Rogers and W. Bel Air Ave. to thank the Lord for protecting us as we walked in the wee hours of the morning. In the dark, quiet morning, I heard a click, so I thought. I made Chariot sit and I slowed my breathing and listened intently. A few minutes later I heard it again and realized that it was the traffic light that clicked as it changed. This time the click was immediately followed by Psalms 46:10 Let be and be still, and know (recognize and understand) that I am God. I will be exalted among the nations! I will be exalted in the earth!

This has always been a favorite verse of mine. I had just finished doing a detailed study on this verse, so it hit me like a ton of bricks. To be still means, without sound, thought or movement. Ironically God had to create sound in Chariot and movement in me, for me to hear, be still and recognize that He is God.

Being an Ambassador of God, wife, mother and Grammy, that verse has spoken peace to my soul many of days, even as a single Mom. This verse has helped me to breathe when I thought that I wouldn't, breathe when I thought that I couldn't and shut up when I didn't want to as well as sit down. Once I succumbed to this verse, it brings peace when I don't know what's ahead, and peace if and when and it normally does, the storm arises. The Lord in His merciful love has a plan for me that has been mapped out before the foundations of the world. Mapped out in Love, that was later displayed on the Cross.

Sometimes we become busy with our lives and the Lord has to draw us in and get our attention like a bad note on a piano or a note sang out of tune to get us back on track... looking unto to Him, the Author and Finisher of our faith. As I look back on those days of walking and running with Chariot before I started my work day, I am so thankful to The Master for teaching me to live my life more abundantly and not waste it. He has taken me from existing to being alive and I am grateful for each day. At times people can and have become irritated with me because of the laughter that I find in things or them. Jesus has placed a merry heart in me and there is nothing that I can or want to do about it. This is the Love of The Savior that He has so graciously shared me and I love sharing it with others.

It was not easy to hear the words stage three cancer associated with my name, because society has labeled it as a death sentence, but sin and disobedience or ending up in eternity without Jesus is a far greater cry of a death sentence than cancer, for He shall deliver me from the snare of the fowler and the noisome pestilence that stalks in darkness (Ps. 91).

Cancer may take for now, my strength, my hair, my appearance, my sleep, my appetite, my immune system, my memory, my endurance as well as other things but it can't take my strength in Christ, my peace, my friendships, my joy, my love, my rest in Christ, my desire for The Word, the remembrance that His Mercy endures, that I am loved with an everlasting love, that I am a royal priesthood, a holy nation, a daughter of the creator, the apple of His eye, dearly beloved, saved by grace, engrafted into the body, fearfully and wonderfully made, chosen, forgiven, excepted in the beloved, sealed til the day of redemption, a Product of His Mercy, healed, delivered, and changed.

2 Corinthians 4:7 However, we possess this precious treasure [the divine Light of the Gospel] in [frail, human] vessels of earth, that the grandeur and exceeding greatness of the power may be shown to be from God and not from ourselves...

THIS IS THE AIR THAT I BREATHE!!!

THESE SHOES ARE MADE FOR WALKING

Growing up as a child, any shoe that touched my foot was a hand me down. As a young married, when possible I shopped bargain basement and depending on what my family needs were, I didn't always have the funds to keep up the heels of my shoes. As the children got older, the Lord gave me wisdom in caring for my footwear. I have shoes that are more than 10 years old but they appear to be 10 days old. When shoes are taken care of, they will help take care of your feet, protecting them.

Ephesians 6th chapter gives us a description for being battle ready. Over and over it mentions the word stand. Back in our day, when a young infant was showing signs of standing, the parents would purchase hard bottom shoes, preferably high tops to support the ankles thereby helping the child to stand. Now we have babies decked out in the latest gear, growing up to be adolescents that refuse to stand for anything. Sorry back on track.

In the biblical days sandals were worn quite a bit, with

the exception of going into battle. During battle time the footwear was extended to cover and protect the shins and calf. If you have ever taken a blow to the shin than you understand the importance of the protecting these areas of the body and how the wearing of this battle ready footwear can help us to stand.

Which brings me to the question, are my gospel shoes, are my battle shoes in better condition than my physical shoes?

The only way that this can be possible for my gospel shoes is that they must come out of the box in living and sharing. They cannot sit on the shelf waiting for that banquet, wedding or family outing. They must be worn into the light of day and sometimes night, become dusty, wet and used in order to help me to stand.

When the fiery darts of the wicked one come, I must not become a turn coat and use them to run, but they must be tied tight for the fight!

What do your shoes look like? Are they neatly keep in a box, free from dirt? Or are they well worn, scuff marks from being slummed in someone's door or the toes worn from pounding the pavement? Are they broken in and comfortable because they remember the path that He has taken? Do they offer the support needed that will help you to stand and fight and resist and share?

Let us all check out our shoes today. They should be like the physical shoes of the Israelites...they must not wear out!

MARTIN LUTHER (KING)

How long, that was a question that Dr. King had back in the 60's. It was also a question in my heart to the Lord on last week.

Back in May of this year, even before my diagnosis, I believed and still do, that my husband has prayed for my healing more than I myself have. It's not that I don't believe or trust God to do so, but that is just the way it is and I won't deny it.

After again making appointments for scans, I took a deep breath and asked the Lord in my heart, How long? After questioning Him, I immediately felt bad because the Holy Spirit gently reminded me of Billy's favorite verse which is Know you not that your body is not your own, but the TEMPLE of God. Then I felt bad for feeling bad, I felt bad for questioning Him. To make myself feel better, on the following day, I laid in bed and watched a Hart to Hart marathon and my husband and son, not knowing about my feelings were super nice to me.

On that evening as I walked thru the living room, my

eyes caught a needlepoint that I'd made more than 25 years ago. Stenciled on the cloth are the words from Hebrews 12:1...THEREFORE THEN, since we are surrounded by so great a cloud of witnesses [who have borne testimony to the Truth], let us strip off and throw aside every encumbrance (unnecessary weight) and that sin which so readily (deftly and cleverly) clings to and entangles us, and let us run with patient endurance and steady and active persistence the appointed course of the race that is set before us.

The word endurance leap out at me and stuck. Across the top of the needlepoint I placed four ladies running a race. With the word endurance in my heart, my mind then went to my Half Marathon and the pain that I experienced and endured to finish this race, which was completely opposite of the fun that I had while rising early and training.

Now before any race, whether 5k, 10k, Half Marathon, Marathon, or Triathlon, once you sign up for the race and pay for it, you are given a course to help get your bearings and gear up your mind as to where you are going and where you should end up. This course is complete with Port a Potty placements, food and water stands and Medical stands. The only thing that isn't listed are the hoards of crazies that show up with signage, music, costumes, pets, you name it, they are there standing on the side lines cheering you on and some even running a few yards with you just to encourage you...to endure.

Endurance, why do I or anyone need endurance? Wikipedia describes endurance as the ability of an organism to remain active for a long period of time, as well as its ability to resist, withstand, recover from and have immunity to trauma, wounds or fatigue. If endurance were a job application I could show up at the interview without showering, brushing my teeth or getting dressed and obtain the job and a pay raise all in the same week.

On Sunday, as I sat in church and watched and listened to those around me serving and ministering, I felt powerless to be able to do the same. Sometimes when I just think about doing something, because of the energy that it requires to think, I need a nap. The Holy Spirit, thank God for Him reminded me that I had taking my eyes of of Jesus. Once I repented the Lord reminded me of what I can do and as I thanked Him, I became grateful, for the feet and legs that at this time cannot run but can walk and carry me, the hands and arms that for right now cannot bench press, but drops my cell phone multiple times during the day, but I have a back that binds to pick it up and eyes that can see where it's fallen. I have millions of saints praying earnestly on my behalf and encouraging me to "endure". I have a God, The Only Wise God, Nobody Greater. A God whose loving kindness is better than life. A God whose mercies are renewed everyday and Great is His faithfulness. I am privileged to be an ambassador of Jehovah Jireh, One Who sees the need before it arise and then He supplies.

Years ago when Pastor Nate had to preach at a church in town the church was equipped with Omnidirectional Microphones. Trinise and the choir members went crazy with what are they called and we need them. The microphones have the ability to pick up the slightest sound and movement and project it whether you are positioned right in front of it or not.

Running this race with Christ, we have a map but unlike the physical race, because Christ payed the price,

He holds the plans and the course, and does not supply us with a turn list. The course is not the same for everyone. The stands to provide our needs are there for us in this race but they aren't pinpointed before we start our race, they are more omnidirectional. No matter where we are Christ, He is in tune with our every sound and movement (Psalms 139:7-16). He knows when I need a rest stop, a banana break, a blood transfusion, a nap, chemo, rebuke, grace for the race, refreshing, solitude, a sleepless nite, a son with a Traumatic Brain Injury, a text, a phone call, a silly friend, healing, a protective dog, a 6'6" husband, a raining day, a stormy nite, beauty for ashes, a portabella mushroom, a designated driver....HE KNOWS!

So, how long is not as important as us running the race, our race with patient endurance and steady and active persistence the appointed course of the race that is set before us.

http://youtu.be/7cK4LrG2tIw

DARK SHADOWS

Psalms 91:1

HE WHO dwells in the secret place of the Most High shall remain stable and fixed under the shadow of the Almighty [Whose power no foe can withstand].

Psalms 23:4

Yes, though I walk through the [deep, sunless] valley of the shadow of death, I will fear or dread no evil, for You are with me; Your rod [to protect] and Your staff [to guide], they comfort me.

Colossians 2:17

Such [things] are only the shadow of things that are to come, and they have only a symbolic value. But the reality (the substance, the solid fact of what is foreshadowed, the body of it) belongs to Christ.

Over 20 years ago, I made a trip to White Marsh Mall one night with Mrs. White, Trinise and Roslyn. Billy and Leslie accompanied us. It was near closing time at the mall and we were in a hurry. The delay came as we walked across the parking lot and Leslie saw her shadow and became hysterical. I tried to get her to touch her shadow. I tried to show her that we all had one. I showed her that I could step on it and it could not hurt her. I tried to show her that it was behind her. With each attempt at calming my hysterical baby, she refused to be quieted.

There are many verses in the bible speaking of or making reference to the word shadow. In Psalms 91:1 shadow speaks of the protection of God and Him defending His children. In Psalms 23:4 shadow speaks of extreme distress; calamity.

Colossians 2:17 shadow represents a sketch or outline. An image cast by an object and representing the form of that object.

Back at the Mall parking lot, when 2 year old Leslie saw her shadow, it became her focus. Knowing that I love her was not enough to make her take her focus off of her shadow. Me jumping into action showing her signs and wonders was not enough for her to take her focus off of her shadow. Me stepping on her shadow was not enough to make her take her focus off of her shadow.

At 2 years old Leslie was immature, being the adult, the mature one, I sought to direct her on a better path. Leslie being immature found it impossible to take her eyes off of her shadow, which became a present danger to her. I chose to focus on my love for her and to show her that "her present danger" was just what it was, a shadow, an image cast.

In this life there are many "shadows" that will and have frightened the very life out of us, simply because we refuse to take our focus off of them making them appear larger than life itself. They pose such a threat that like little Leslie, it stops us in our tracks, complete with crying, screaming and pulling away from the source of our protection.

Psalms 91:1 speaks of the protection of God for His children. When the shadows of Ps. 23:4 shows up, you know, the calamity and distress, if we are abiding in the Most High, then the Shadow of the Almighty becomes our protection.

There is one other thing that I tried to show Leslie and that is the lamppost overhead that was causing her little body to cast its image. If we will only look up to the light and make it our focus and not the shadow. Christ has shown His love for us by dying on the cross, thereby stepping on our shadow (death) and removing its sting and yet we still on a daily basis become fearful of the shadow.

Today, while it is called today, lets make a conscience effect to look towards the Light, and dwell in the secret place of The Most High and remain stable and fixed under the shadow of The Almighty...Whose power no foe can withstand !!!

http://youtu.be/eM_JRAPSwVM

THE F WORD

As I look back over my various blogs, to encourage myself. Back in early April, I ended one particular blog with a scripture, Hebrews 10:23 which reads, So let us seize and hold fast and retain without wavering the hope we cherish and confess and our acknowledgement of it, for He Who promised is reliable (sure) and faithful to His word.

For the past several months, my heart was excited just thinking over the blessings that the Lord had prepared just for my family. I have been looking forward to Thanksgiving with a grateful heart. The night of October 12th, I had fractioned sleep. The dog had an upset stomach and I was excited that the following day at chemo was a new day for me...an answer to prayer. As I sat on the couch late that night with my IPad, I listened to a sermon from several weeks prior when I'd missed Sunday morning worship service. The title of Pastor Steves's message was, What happens when your dream dies? The message was taken from 2 Kings 4th chapter. The message added to the gratefulness that I was experiencing.

With several hours of sleep under my belt, I showered and dressed to head to the hospital. Once I check in and my blood is drawn, normally within 10mins, the drugs are attached to my port for administering. On this particular day 10, 20 30 and now 40 minutes have passed and I'm still waiting. Finally after almost an hour, my meds are ready. After about 3 minutes of receiving meds, I receive a call from my cousin asking of my whereabouts. His next comment shook me, Your house is on FIRE. Now the words house is on fire is one thing but the other is that this was the only day that Billy was left home.

My heart raced and pounded, my brain thought that I weighed too much so in order to correct the problem, it told my bowels to empty themselves...5 times. As Bill headed home and I stayed at the hospital, I prayed and phoned Billy numerous times...with no answer. There was a myriad of emotions, prayers, scripture and phone calls going on.

Within about 15 or 20 minutes, I spoke to Billy on the phone and my heart was settled. What shape the house was in did not matter. A short span later Bill called me several times, during one of his calls he said, the dog is fine. Now anyone who knows me, knows how I feel about my dog but yet and still she never entered my thought pattern during this process.

God in His Sovereignty, had ordained Bill and I to be at the hospital, and Billy to be in the house when His plan unfolded.. Seemingly 500 phone calls later at about 1am, my family and I, the dog included settled into a hotel room. He, the Holy Spirit brought to my attention that if it had not been for Jesus, that I would not be able to seize and hold fast to my faith, because I have no power in myself to do anything. Ironically, in medical terms, hold fast is something to which something else may be firmly secured. While my meds were firmly attached to me, I had to be firmly attached to my faith in order not to loose it. I had to not waver about my purpose, the thing to be attained, due to the fact that this is the faith that I both hold dear and acknowledge, for God Who is both capable and reliable is faithful to His Word!

TOUCHED

As Pastor Steve preached on Sunday, he said that Jesus was touched wth the feeling of my infirmities. Touched with the feeling of my infirmities. It stuck in my mind, the importance of this verse.

When I went to have my first CT Scan the technician was extremely comforting with her words and actions toward me. I couldn't help but think how trained she was at performing her job. About 3 months later when I had to have another CT Scan, the technician looked at me and says, I remember you and my heart broke when I thought about all that I went through, knowing that you were about to face the same things, how are you Honey?

She too, like Christ had been "affected" with the same frailties as I have. Touched with the feelings of my infirmities. It amazes me that the triune God, that became man, has been touched with the feelings of all of my infirmities...yet without sin.

There was a popular commercial that aired during the late 80's, early 90's. Its advantage was Sy Sperling saying,

I'm not just the president of Hair Club for Men, I'm also a client. Then Sy showed us a picture of himself before the transplant.

I have always loved the book of Hebrews. It gives us not a picture, but an entire photo album of Christ. Starting out with Him being The Appointed Heir, Owner and Creator of all things. The Express Image of the Father. A better Intercessor and Priest and ending with Him being Jesus, that Great Shepherd of the sheep.

I don't know about you, but I'm having a hard time picking my favorite picture of Christ. As Creator, everything that He made, He said was good, with the exception of man, which He said was very good and capped it off with fearfully and wonderfully made. As Intercessor, He speaks on behalf of me so that I receive mercies renewed every day and not the punishment that I deserve. As Priest, He will diagnosis, prescribe and heal me all in the same breath. As my Great Shepherd, when I carry the latest and greatest GPS on full charge, He steps in and leads and guides me, becoming a lamp unto my feet and a light unto my pathway.

Now if a human being, unsaved or saved can have compassion on me because of the afflictions shared. How much more shall The God of the Universe, Who has been "touched with the feeling of my infirmities?"

This is one of the great advantages of the Lord. I'm not sure about you, but I'll take the entire album, one snapshot of Christ is not enough for me... I need Him for all of my infirmities!

Hebrews 4:15

For we do not have a High Priest Who is unable to

understand and sympathize and have a shared feeling with our weaknesses and infirmities and liability to the assaults of temptation, but One Who has been tempted in every respect as we are, yet without sinning.

NOT FOR THE FAINT
AT HEART

My husband reminded the congregation, several weeks ago during his message how much I love living outside of the box. Inside of the box reminds me of a cage. There are limitations to your movement, your vision, and your abilities. Outside of the box, I think of a bird being released from its cage.

Early into our marriage, during the month of late September, early October, Bill and I got dressed to head out and he looked at me with alarm in his eyes and said, "you can't wear white after Labor Day." My reply was simple, yes I can.

Now I know that some of you, that are comfortable in your box is reading this and cringing and agreeing with my hubby.

Another trend that makes some people cringe is wearing stripes. Let me give you a hand. If you want to look svelte, don't wear horizontal stripes as they tend to add bulk. Mixing prints with patterns may be a bit much. Wear stripes with jeans or a black bottom, both items pairs well with everything right. Wear stripes with a neutral color if you want to feel safe. Vertical stripes can make you appear taller which is good if you are vertically challenged like myself. Don't wear clown socks with pinstripe pants and last a pinstripe suit is always on point. You can feel free to use these pointers in your wearing of stripes or you can step outside of the box like Someone else that I know.

Now whether white after Labor Day or stripes with patterns, they are all some type of clothing. At the scourging of Christ leading up to His crucifixion, all clothing was removed. In Jewish law 39 stripes or blows were given. With Jesus there is no record of how many blows were received by Him. The whip that was used was made of bone and metal and was attached to strips of leather. This beating not only removed the skin from His body, but the tissue and muscle was ripped from His bone as well. Anyone receiving such a flogging usually lost consciousness and sometimes died from the beating itself. But Christ, My Savior, after He received His beating, He was made to carry His cross, uphill, afterward being nailed to it. He cared not that His stripes made Him look bulky, too tall, fashionable, like a clown or going too far because He was outside of the box.

He knows that He is the Creator of that box and as He looked at and received each blow, He saw you and I in need of a healing, saving, Savior. Each stripe whether horizontal, vertical or diagonal was proudly worn all the way to the grave.

On the upper right portion of my chest, I have a 2 inch scar from the installation of my port. I've always hated that scar, which will be visible during warmer weather. A 2 inch scar, which I can cover up at my choosing. But Christ proudly wore His stripes all the way up Golgatha's hill.

Isaiah 53:5

But He was wounded for our transgressions, He was bruised for our guilt and iniquities; the chastisement [needful to obtain] peace and well-being for us was upon Him, and with the stripes [that wounded] Him we are healed and made whole.

SPRING TIME

Spring time, my second most favorite time of year. My first, summer. I love summer time for the simple fact that I can dig and plant and decorate my garden to be a most beautiful landscape on the outside of my home. As I drive down the street I can see the work of others as well as their love for gardening and I imagine them choosing flowers and deciding where to plant them. Shade plants, sun plants, perrinials, annuals, blues, reds, yellows, flower boxes, plants that like wet feet, trailers, morning glories, moon beams, mulch. Ahhhh summertime!

This year at 6:45pm on March 20th Spring is scheduled to arrive. It's time to start looking for those bulbs that were planted in the fall to peep thru the snow. That which has lain dead all winter is now yawning and coming to life. First the tiny green leaves appear and my heart skips a beat. It's like a royal announcement to me. What color will it be? Are there others or did you come alone? Will you survive the frost if it returns? I wonder if the neighbors plants are growing? I get all twitter pated!

Summer, she is scheduled to arrive at 12:38pm on June 21ˢᵗ. School closing, longer days and nights, swimming pools, cold treats and my favorite...AIR CONDITIONING.

We all have our favorite time or times of year and look forward to there arrival, even checking the calendar as if to ensure that they arrive on time. How much more differently would we live our lives if our favorite time of year never arrived or if the equator where to shift and our season would show up arbitrarily?

Would you change the clothes around in your closet, wax your car? Would you buy mulch and salt at the same time? Take down your sheers and put up drapes? Would you wear your winter coat in June, shorts in December? Or would you live your life in utter kaos because of the uncertainty of the season or would you realize that CHRIST is still the Alpha and Omega and that there is nothing new under the sun.

The bible speaks of various times and seasons. God tells the Israelites to remember the month Abib with a celebration...The Feast of Unleavened Bread. It is the first month and it will not change (Exodus 34:18). In the New Testament we learn that in due time (season) CHRIST died for the ungodly (Romans 5:6). That should give us Joy, but the one that gives us the most grief is Due Season. God tells us that in Due Season, we will reap if we faint not (Gal. 6:9). I've checked the bible, Google, Bing, Yahoo and even the Farmer's Almanac and none of them can pinpoint for me the arrival of Due Season. The ironic thing is is that it may not even be in this calendar year....for me!

Why would God just throw that in there, due time?

Let's back the bus up a bit. Perfect Adam and Eve,

living in paradise...sinned...God foreclosed on their home. No refinancing, no reworking the loan, bank owned. God gave them sons, Cain n Abel. Cain kills Abel, price on his head. Sodom and Gomorrah destroyed...homosexuality. Imagination of man's heart...wicked...God gives Noah n his family a ride on The Love Boat saving only him and his family...animals included. Famine in the land....Joseph to the rescue, Pharaoh dies, in steps Pharaoh who knew not Joseph. Gods people in bondage, in comes Moses, bloody waters, flies, death, Red Sea....wilderness. Fast forward a bit through Joshua, Judges, David's life, Ruth, Hosea and all the way to the end of the Old Testament and and let's take a ferry to the New Testament. What was that in between the Old n the New? You say you didn't hear anything...well neither did the people. Four hunet (an yes I said hunet, not hundred) years of SILENCE! NOTHING FROM GOD... NOTHING! And we feel that we have the right to know when due season is? Due season is when God says it is. Many of us are growing weary from wanting to know when due season is, when our concentration should be on "the doing well" that prompts God to bless us in "due season". Doing well, my business...due season, God"s business.

SAUL

Saul of Tarsus was thee worse, or thee best depending on what you are looking at. If you look at it from Paul's point of view, being a Jew, he was an upstanding law abiding citizen.

Circumcised the eighth day, of the stock of Israel, of the tribe of Benjamin, an Hebrew of the Hebrews; as touching the law, a Pharisee; Concerning zeal, persecuting the church; touching the righteousness which is in the law, blameless (Phil. 3:5-6).

If you look at it through the eyes of a Christian that lived during Saul's days, he was the worse. Listen to what Saul says about himself. Which thing I also did in Jerusalem: and many of the saints did I shut up in prison, having received authority from the chief priests; and when they were put to death, I gave my voice against them. And I punished them oft in every synagogue, and compelled them to blaspheme; and being exceedingly mad against them, I persecuted them even unto strange cities (Acts 26:10-11).

Saul was present during the stoning of Stephen And cast him out of the city, and stoned him: and the witnesses laid down their clothes at a young man's feet, whose name was Saul (Acts 7:58). He even consented unto Stephen's death, while he was preaching the gospel (Acts 8:1a).

Saul was very proficient at what he did. A Hebrew of the Hebrews, a Pharisee, touching the law blameless, and a killer of Christians!

And then one day on the Damascus road when it pleased God, He revealed Himself to Saul. (Gal. 1:15-16)...Not when Stephen was being stoned, not when family members cried as their loved ones were being jailed and or killed, but when it pleased God.

Minister Bill and I are blessed to have four children. When giving birth to these children with Stacey labor was eight hours, Billy four, Leslie 2, and if you're like me you're thinking Douglas would be one hour.

The year 1991 was one of the hottest summers that I remember. The air conditioner had gone up in my 1987 Ford Taurus and the 25 mile drive to the hospital on appointment day was brutal. The doctors gave me the due date of July 16th and for me, the countdown began, as well as other things. Looking back this was the hardest of all of my pregnancies. I was able to exercise well into my seventh month but I felt the weight of carrying this baby. Starting out with a weight of 130, I didn't gain too much weight until maybe the 5th month, which caused people to often say to me, are you sure you're pregnant? After the 5th month the doctors constantly laid into me for gaining too much weight. By the day of delivery, I was a little over 200 pounds. The arches of my feet ached tremendously. I woke up one day with a numbness from my right hip down to my ankle. The doctor confirmed the numbness as a pinched nerve and ordered me to stay off of me feet for several days. I remember waking Minister Bill in the wee hours of the night to carry me to the bathroom. My body ached. With each breath that I took Stacey would say, do you need me to get the suitcase Mom?

As July 16th neared, I became hopeful. A month before my expected date of delivery the doctors started to throw around the idea of a C-section, saying that the baby would be big. I began preparing meals to store in the freezer for Bill, Stacey, Billy and Leslie to have while I was in the hospital with the baby. I would iron outfits for the family, placing them on individual hangers. For the kids each hanger had an outfit complete with socks and undies and a choice of 2 pair of shoes. Something happened...a week prior to my date of expectation the doctors changed my date from July 16th to July 26th. I was so hot, in more ways than one and I decided in my heart, I'll show them by delivering early. A week after July 26th, I was scheduled for an all day stress test in which I passed with flying colors, but still no baby. The technician even commented, this may get things started and don't be surprised when you end up back here at the hospital tonight having this baby. On August 8th I was scheduled for yet another stress test, where the decision was made to induce labor on August the 11th.

Completely exhausted and angry with time, pregnancy, heat, due dates, schedules and a myriad of other things, I returned home. I had began to crack into my freezer stash, there were no more little cute hangers in the kids closets, Min. Bill was preparing for the Tony Evans Evangelism Conference in town. At about 11:00 pm that night, I uttered the words, I think I'm in labor. We arrived at the hospital around 11:30pm. Breathing deeper than ever, pushing harder than ever and praying for this to be over like yesterday, at 5:01am THE NEXT DAY, I had a 10 pound, 24 inch long baby boy.

All of my crying, praying, complaining, hate of heat, exhaustion, planning and preparing changed nothing for me, but....WHEN IT PLEASED GOD!!!

YESTERDAY'S GONE

Yesterday: time in the immediate past. Tomorrow: the day following today. Today: the present day time or age.

1Pet. 5:7 Casting the whole of your care [all your anxieties, all your worries, all your concerns,once and for all] on Him, for He cares for you affectionately and cares about you watchfully.

During the course of my 30 year marriage, (31 yrs in just a few short weeks) I've never been a worrier. Once in a blue moon something would grab my heart, but as a whole on a daily basis, no. Since Billy's divine appointment with God on December 2, 2012, on Roosevelt Blvd. in Philadelphia, I've found myself worrying at different times. This has been a slow, painful, rewarding, learning, terrifying merciful, journey with Jesus...and it's not over.

Living with my parents as a young Christian single mother, one of my favorite bible verses was, to know Him in the power of His resurrection and the fellowship of His sufferings. Today I'm learning that even more so. Like we sang as children, every rung goes higher, higher.. Had The

Lord shown me this portion of my life with Him, I would have bowed out years ago and not so gracefully.

The Lord has lovingly taken the theology out of the verses that I'd committed to heart and He's put some flesh, agony, experience, maturity, and love into those verses.

I've always been the type of person who against hope believed in hope, right off of the bat. But since December 2, 2012, that one day emptied my entire heart savings and everyday I have to "PRESS".

My prayer for you is that you will enjoy that peace that passes all understand, because God promised that it will keep your heart and mind at ease. Do not get caught in yesterday or tomorrow, but remember that THIS IS THE DAY THAT THE LORD HAS MADE AND HE HAS COMMANDED US TO REJOICE AND BE GLAD IN IT.

HIS WAY

The way that he takes me. On yesterday I had the opportunity to spend time in Philly with my kidz. Since Billy lived there for more than 5 years, he will give me a short cut to each destination. On some occasions when I reach the end of a road which he has sent me down I will say, Billy which way next and his answer is I don't know. Then I have to resort to my GPS because his brain has grown tired.

There are several things about the way that he takes me. The streets are small side streets unlike the main streets. They are darker and have a few more bumps than the normal route. It also seems to be a longer route to me but one thing I do know and that is that it always gets me to my destination. At times I want to say to Billy don't worry I got it, just relax. But I understand that in order for his injured brain to continue its healing process it must be exercised in every way possible.

Every time Billy leads me through Philly I think about Jesus leading me. He doesn't take the expressway, He instead takes the narrow way (Matt. 7:13-14). He doesn't take the crowded streets, He chooses the road less traveled. It seems like a longer route to me because I am unfamiliar with this way or even unwilling to take this way in trust. But unlike Billy, Jesus' brain never grows tired. He himself says, Low I am with you always, even unto the ends of the earth. He will never check out on you.

Jesus whispers those words to me that I refrain from saying to Billy. RELAX, cease striving, not only do I know the way but I am the way (John 14:6).

What has injured you in the fellowship that you are not receiving healing for? Could it be that you have ceased exercising that injury but have instead sheltered it for relief? Have you ever given birth, known someone who have had surgery or been that someone that have had surgery? How long did the medical staff allow you to sit or lay because of your condition? How about therapy was that given a year after your illness?

When Billy arrived at Moss Rehab on December 20, 2012, which is by the way 1 of the United States top 10 rehab centers, the process began. He could do nothing more than open his eyes. He literally had absolutely no control over his body. By February 2013, Billy was walking, talking, eating, laughing, crying, playing games, reading, remembering and on and on...HALLELUJAH and MERCI BEAUCOUP! But for him and his family, it has been a long, dark, bumpy, painful, unfamiliar road. But this is the road loaded with healing. And since it is His- story, Jesus', not Billy's, it is the best road for me to take.

As I look back on the past year and a half and The Holy Spirit reminds me that "my light affliction"???? Did He say light??? Yes light affliction cannot not be compared, well He says it best Himself: 2 Corinthians 4:17 For our light, momentary affliction (this slight distress of the passing hour) is ever more and more abundantly preparing and producing and achieving for us an everlasting weight of glory [beyond all measure, excessively surpassing all comparisons and all calculations, a vast and transcendent glory and blessedness never to cease!],

Just like Moss Rehab, Jesus always gives us His best, but we often miss it because we are unwilling to press through the pain.

Not a bad ending for someone that the doctors did not think would live through the night huh. But it is not the ending, it is merely the beginning...wait until you hear him preach!!!

What is your "light affliction"?

BOUND

While we are taking in extra fiber please make sure that our liquid intake has increased. If not our intestines will become bound and we would like them to be free. By now, our 3rd day you may have noticed that your limbs feel a little lighter, your intestines may not feel as "heavy" and your hearing may even appear a little clearer....He that hath an ear, let him hear. Since Elohei Chaseddi: The God of my Mercy, has brought Billy back to our home, I've noticed the clutter in my house that I never excepted before, be it a room, table top, corner of the floor or whatever the location. The Lord has told me that I have the same type of clutter in my life!. The thing about clutter is that it always seems to be something that is needed right now and that's why it's not put away. But if someone knocks at the door it quickly becomes an eyesore. Well God who tabernacles with us, sees all. For the past few weeks the Lord has told me to GET RID OF THE CLUTTER and don't drag it back out. He says that He is all that I need. The question at hand, will I "HEAR" Him. Will I allow Him to purge me with Hyssop. Hyssop is a medicinal plant with antiseptic properties. Hyssop has also been used to cleanse or stimulate the gastrointestinal system. As our fiber rich foods cleanse our systems, let us bow to the Lord like David when he said, Purify me with Hyssop, and I shall be clean (ceremonially); wash me, and I shall (in reality) be whiter than snow. Purging hurts, hyssop stinks, sin kills and God restores.

So that He might sanctify her, having cleansed her by the washing of water with the Word Eph. 5:26.

WATER

How often and how much water do you drink? Our body is made up of 70% water. Well the lack of water is the cause for some of the health issues that we suffer from, constipation, diarrhea, dry skin, inflammed skin, headaches and achy joints just to name a few. You can receive water from the foods that you eat but it is not enough. Every morning, I drink a cup of hot water with a lemon squeezed into the water. Water washes, cleanses, and it supply's.

At least once a year I receive a letter from the town of Aberdeen telling me that I have a certain level of chemicals and pollutants in my water. That sentence is followed by, "not to worry, it's perfectly safe to drink.????? So I'm really paying to drink poison water. If you had the chance to choose, which would you choose? Acid water, Arsenic Water, Deer Park, Dasani or freshly filtered water in your home? I'm sure that you would choose whatever in your mind is the purest form of water to nourish your body. But, no matter which one you choose Jesus says that all who drinks of this water will thirst again. To the women at the well He says,

"But whoever takes a drink of the water that I shall give (supply) him shall never, no never, be thirsty any more. The woman says to Him, Sir, GIVE me this water, so that I may never get thirsty (John 14:13-15).

For some of us reading we need to be like the women at the well, our response to Jesus should be GIVE me this water, that I may never thirst again. To others we need the daily washing of the water of the Word. Whichever person that we are today, it is the purest form of water that you will ever receive. Again the question at hand is, how much water do you drink? A verse of Psalms? A chapter of Ephesians a week? Five minutes of Charles Stanley a day? Or Pastor Nate on Sundays and Wednesdays and Min. Bill Moultrie on Sunday Mornings? Today my prayer is that we will "hear" the Lord's call to leave the dry and thirsty land where no water is, to see His power and His might! Allow the Lord to sanctify you with the washing of the Water of His Word. DRINK UP!!!

SIXTH DAY,

God said, Let us (Father, Son, Holy Spirit) make mankind in Our image, after Our likeness, and let them have complete authority over the fish of the sea, the birds of the air, the (tame) beasts, and over all of the earth, and over everything that creeps upon the earth.

So God created man in His own image, in the likeness of God He created him; male and female He created them.

And God blessed them and said to them, Be fruitful, multiply, and fill the earth, and subdue it (using all its vast resources in the service of God and man); and have dominion over the fish of the sea, the air, and over every living creature that moves upon the earth.

And God said, See, I have given you every plant yielding seed that is on the face of all the land and every tree with seed in its fruit; you shall have them for food.

And to all the animals on the earth and to every bird of the air and to everything that creeps on the ground-to everything in which there is the breath of life-I have given every green plant for food. And it was so.

And God saw everything that He had made, and behold, it was very good (suitable, pleasant) and He approved it completely. And there was evening and there was morning, a sixth day. Genesis 1:26-31

I find it amazing that God created mankind to have "dominion" over the beast, everything that creeps, swims, flies and the like in its living state but once it's dead and we add a little heat, oil and salt n pepper, IT has dominion over us! Dominion: to rule, dominate, subjugate. The other that amazes me is that he gave us trees w/fruit and plants bringing forth seed for fruit and we seem to omit that in our daily eating. So in your eating of everything that is not meat and or fried in oil, know that you are in the will of the Father who created you on THE SIXTH DAY!

On this sixth day of fasting continue to glorify God by eating your whole grains, fruits and veggies and drinking your water. As we are cleaned out physically allow the Word of God to clean us out spiritually so that the fruit of the Spirit will be evident in our lives. Then we will be able to bring forth fruit, more fruit, much fruit, and fruit that remains.

As much as I love my hubby, before I am his wife, before I am the mother of Stacey, Billy, Leslie and Douglas, whom I also love, I am an Ambassador of Christ. I should look, smell and sound like I am from the country of Heaven, although I have yet to see It. But since I am to represent the one Who sent me and His Spirit resides in me and He resides in Heaven, then that is who and what I should look like.

Contribute to the need's of God's people (sharing in the necessities of the saints); pursue the practice of hospitality.

Bless those who persecute you (who are cruel in their attitude toward you); bless and do not curse them.

Rejoice with those who rejoice (sharing others' joy), and weep with those who weep (sharing others' grief).

Live in harmony with one another; do not be haughty (snobbish, high-minded, exclusive), but readily adjust yourself to (people, things) and give yourselves to humble tasks. Never overestimate yourself or be wise in your own conceits

Repay no one evil for evil, but take thought for what is honest and proper and noble (aiming to be above reproach) in the sight of everyone.

If possible, as far as depends on you, live at peace with everyone.

Beloved, never avenge yourselves, but leave the way open for (God's) wrath; for it is written, Vengeance is Mine, I will repay (requite), says The Lord.

But if your enemy is hungry, feed him; if he is thirsty, give him drink; for by so doing you will heap burning coals upon his head.

Do not let yourself be overcome with evil, but overcome (master) evil with good. Romans 12:13-21

PUT ON YOUR SHOES AND LACE THEM UP TIGHT, THERE'S WORK TO BE DONE!!!

FOCUS

During this past fall Billy and I left therapy and headed for the fast food choice for his lunch for that day. As we sat in line in the drive through, I read and laughed at a bumper sticker on the car ahead of us. When I asked him to read it he could not even see the sticker. Three days later at the eye doctor, I cried as I found that my son who previously wore reading glasses could not even see the largest of letters on the optical chart. His entire world was out of focus and I had know idea.

How is your eyesight? Is what you think that you see, really what you see? What are you looking at? Can you not see the forrest for the trees?

I saw the movie the Passion of Christ for the first time about 5 years ago in Ghana, West Africa. The movie gives us a literal picture of Isaiah 53. I cried as I watched and wondered how could Christ continue on with such torture? What kind of love would carry him this far? Hebrews 12:2 reads, Looking away [from all that will distract] to Jesus,

Who is the Leader and the Source of our faith [giving the first incentive for our belief] and is also its Finisher [bringing it to maturity and perfection]. He, for the joy [of obtaining the prize] that was set before Him, endured the cross, despising and ignoring the shame, and is now seated at the right hand of the throne of God. WOW! The joy of obtaining the prize set before Him. The prize, that's you and I. He endured. He bravely and calmly beared up under everything that was thrown at Him. He despised and ignored the shame. He thought little or really nothing of the dishonor of sin that he was bearing, because He had His eye on the "prize". What focus!

So on this 7th day of fasting as well as Communion Sunday, what or where is our focus? Are we yet digging into our closet for the item that was too snug a week ago? Are we thinking about the Colossal Coronary Clogger(burger) that we are eating when this in done? Are we excited about Easter this year because He arose or because we can go back to our old ways of eating? Or are we excited about the healing of relationships and the breaking of sin in our lives that will not be passed onto the next generation?

FOCUS...ATTENTION...

HUNGRY

Matthew 4:2-4

And He went without food for forty days and forty nights, and later He was hungry.

And the tempter came and said to Him, If You are God's Son, command these stones to be made [loaves of] bread.

But He replied, It has been written, Man shall not live and be upheld and sustained by bread alone, but by every word that comes forth from the mouth of God.

Matthew 4:8-9

Again, the devil took Him up on a very high mountain and showed Him all the kingdoms of the world and the glory (the splendor, magnificence, preeminence, and excellence) of them.

And he said to Him, These things, all taken together, I will give You, if You will prostrate Yourself before me and do homage and worship me.

As Jesus fasted, the bible says that "later", He became hungry...later. Did you become hungry as soon as the fast started, or later. Did the tempter come and tell you to turn your beans into steak, your salad into fish or your Pad Thai into Chicken Alfredo? After you realized your hunger, like Jesus, did you turn to the Word?

Several things about these passages stick out to me. One is that Satan offered Jesus what already belonged to Him, more ironically, that which He created. Satan does the same with us, offers us what is already ours if we worship Him. God has given us all things that pertain to life and Godliness (2 Peter 1:3). But due to our lack of fellowship with God and or our lack of "exercised faith",we don't catch it.

The other is that when tempted, The Word turned to The Word for strength! That blows my mind every time I read it and yet I fail to do it so many times, which results in a failure of strength.

Why didn't CHRIST just reach deep inside of Himself and pull out the strength that He needed. I believe that it had to do with this word called "submission". And after He had appeared in human form, He abased and humbled Himself [still further] and carried His obedience to the extreme of death, even the death of the cross! (Phil. 2:8).

If we but submit ourselves to the Father! I can only imagine. Phil. 2:8 tells us that because of the submission of CHRIST to the Father, we and countless numbers have received salvation...because of Christ's refusal to turn the stones and worship Satan.

Prayerfully we have learned that this fast was not for me to pick out the splinter in your eye and vice versa, but rather for each of us to submit himself to God who judges righteously.

When He was reviled and insulted, He did not revile or

offer insult in return; [when] He was abused and suffered, He made no threats [of vengeance]; but he trusted [Himself and everything] to Him Who judges fairly (1 Peter 2:23).

Let your light SHINE today! "Lighthouses don't fire cannons to call attention to their shining-they just shine."- D.L. Moody

Wanda Moultrie

SUFFERING

A little over 10 years ago, my husband was teaching Wednesday Night Bible Study. He'd given us the homework of making a list of two things. One was some of the gifts that God gives, the other was gifts that we personally possess.

I remember that on my list for possession, I'd listed suffering. When I raised my hand to tell the class, on the faces of those present, there were frozen expressions, mumbles of that's not a gift and heads shaking left to right.

The verse that I used and still stick by today is 1 Peter 4:19 Therefore, those who are ill-treated and suffer in accordance with God's will must do right and commit their souls [in charge as a deposit] to the One Who created [them] and will never fail [them].

Too many times when someone is "going through", they are looked at as if they are in sin and when that view is taken, it hinders the way that we minister to them, if at all.

While we can and do suffer because of sin, either ours or the sins of someone else, we also suffer so that God's glory can be revealed. Remember the blind man, Jesus was asked the question, "who sinned, him or his parents. Jesus' answer, neither this man or his parents, but that his blindness was for the glory of God (John 9: 2-3).

There may be one, but right now I can't think of any gift that my husband has given me that I have not displayed. When I make use of the exercise equipment that he purchased for me, I am displaying his gift. When I drive down the road, I am displaying his gift of a Ford Expedition. When I cook my Daniel approved meals, I am displaying his gift of electricity running through my home, the gift of food, pots and pans, as well as God's gift of the knowledge and strength to cook.

God commanded us to be "good stewards" of what He has given us and to "exercise" our gifts. How are you displaying your gifts from the Master, for the Master?

2 Timothy 2:3

Take [with me] your share of the hardships and suffering [which you are called to endure] as a good (first-class) soldier of Christ Jesus.

2 Timothy 3:12

Indeed all who delight in piety and are determined to live a devoted and godly life in Christ Jesus will meet with persecution [will be made to suffer because of their religious stand].

1 Peter 4:12-13

Beloved, do not be amazed and bewildered at the fiery ordeal which is taking place to test your quality, as though something strange (unusual and alien to you and your position) were befalling you.

But insofar as you are sharing Christ's sufferings, rejoice, so that when His glory [full of radiance and splendor] is revealed, you may also rejoice with triumph [exultantly].

Matthew 5:10

Blessed and happy and enviably fortunate and spiritually prosperous(in the state in which the born-again child of God enjoys and finds satisfaction in God's favor and salvation, regardless of his outward conditions) are those who are persecuted for righteousness' sake (for being and doing right), for theirs is the kingdom of heaven!

Philippians 3:10-11

[For my determined purpose is] that I may know Him [that I may progressively become more deeply and intimately acquainted with Him, perceiving and recognizing and understanding the wonders of His Person more strongly and more clearly], and that I may in that same way come to know the power outflowing from His resurrection [which it exerts over believers], and that I may so share His sufferings as to be continually transformed [in spirit into His likeness even] to His death, [in the hope]

That if possible I may attain to the [spiritual and moral] resurrection [that lifts me] out from among the dead [even while in the body].

Wanda Moultrie

THE PROGRAM

My husband often teases me because at times I like to watch the ID channel. For those of you that are unaware, that's Investigative Discovery.

Occasionally when someone witnesses a murder and are called on to testify, the life of the witness becomes threatened.

Witness protection is usually required were law enforcement sees a risk for the witnesses to be intimidated by colleagues or defendants. The program can place a single individual or an entire family under protection. The person making the threat must have the resources, intent and motivation to carry out the threat. Once this is determined, funds are dispersed by the program for the safety and protection of the individuals.

Although the program is for safety and protection, one can be quickly uprooted from home, family, friends and all that is comfortable to perfectly new surroundings. It can be very abrupt and somewhat disturbing for those under protection.

When Joseph had come to his brothers, they stripped him of his [distinctive] long garment which he was wearing; Then they took him and cast him into the [well-like] pit which was empty; there was no water in it, Genesis 37:23-24.

I can't imagine his feelings. Suddenly going from being the apple of his daddy's eye playing while his brothers worked, to being placed in a pit.

As a result of Judah being an awe-inspiring salesmen, Joseph was sold to the Midianites for 20 pieces of silver and they in turn sold him to Potiphar. Joseph received what is known as an S-6 visa...he was an alien.

Joseph's colleagues, known as his brothers have now become the defendants. His brothers hated him and were jealous of him. Genesis 37:4-5, 11. And amazingly it was all a part of God's plan.

Now Joseph had not witnessed a crime, but since God is omniscient, He had to protect Joseph for His program. He sent His very best to be with Joseph, he was not alone. God Himself was with Joseph every step of the way, Genesis 39:1-3.

Have you ever been in a pit that came upon you suddenly...at the hands of your own brothers? Have they been jealous of you, hated you. FEAR NOT! You may be in God's Witness Protection Program.

Joseph's story got much worse before it got better. All in all, Joseph became angry but he never became bitter. He was able years later to look his brothers in the eye, with tears in his eyes and declare, As for you, you thought evil against me, but God meant it for good, to bring about that many people should be kept alive, as they are this day. Genesis 50:20.

Just thinking about some of my pits, they can be cold, lonely, dark, scary, seemingly never ending and costly. But The Master, has A Master Plan. Take a cue from Joseph... be angry and sin not and like Joseph you may live to see the unfolding of God's plan after your protection.

God's protection over Joseph was so extreme that even Joseph's bones received protection, Joshua 24:32.

http://youtu.be/n03dGuJm7XM

Wanda Moultrie

THE JOURNEY BEGINS

Back in January of 2013, I was diagnosed with diverticulitis. Some nights were very hard me. I would sit on the couch drinking baking soda and water while praying for relief. I sought remedies by changing when I ate, where I ate, how much and what. The best relief for me was to not eat out and cut out as many "preservatives" as possible. Ironically the lack of preservatives gave me the best comfort. I found that those preservatives were preserving the foods from spoilage while at the same time causing my spoilage.

I did cleanses, which always left me feeling revived, freer in my digestive system and more in control of my health. September of 2014, I became a vegetarian and have never looked back. February of 2015 I deleted soda from my life. Canada Dry Ginger Ale was my love. When I go into the drink aisle in Walmart, I hear my girl Dionne Warwick singing "Walk on By."

May of 2015, I was diagnosed with "Inflammatory Breast Cancer", which is very rare. If you take 100 women that actually have breast cancer, only 1 of them will have

Inflammatory. So I am in the 1% of women with this disease. I am in stage 3 being that the disease mask itself as an infection and it does not show up on a mammogram. So as today will be to others June 9, 2015, it will always be to me, my first day of Chemo.

Chemo is a combination of drugs used to treat cancer. The combination varies with each diagnosis. Take me, I am estrogen negative and HER2 positive meaning that the cancer is not driven by estrogen, but contains extra Protein. So the doctors will mix chemicals specifically for that diagnosis. The goal is to stop or slow the growth of cancer cells.

Within the past month, I have visited various doctors at least 30 times, sometimes 2 or 3 in one day. At times I left more hurt and bruised than when I arrived. All I could do when I returned home was to rest.

Christ has a Chemo lab for us too and He has promised that if we run to Him in our time of need, when something doesn't seem normal or right or off kilter, that in His lab, he will

Cleanse us with
Hyssop in order to
Empower us to
Minister
On Demand

Have you ever thought about the cleansing cycle in a washing machine. Twisting, turning, pulling, with a mixing of water and chemicals. In the Old Testament, Hyssop was used for cleaning and purifying. Several years ago I took a bottle of hyssop to church and asked Pastor Nate to smell it. I refused to tell him what it was. He was appalled that

that scent was in his nostrils. When Billy was injured, I had to gain Power of Authority over his affairs. I was then empowered to legally act on his behalf. A minister is one who is authorized to perform certain duties.

Five years ago Min. Bill and I made our first missionary trip together to Ghana, West Africa, I like the sound of that. On our first mission while there, all missionaries present gathered and boarded the back end of a tractor which was pulled by a tractor and headed hours out thru the jungle to the village. Once we arrived, we made ourselves friendly with the children as the parents had not yet returned home from their manual labor and their minimum of 3 hr walk home. We received the massage that they were on their way. About 4 or 5 hrs later when they began to slowly arrive, it was pitch black. Not I didn't pay my electric bill dark, not even the power is out in the neighborhood for a few days due to a storm. I'm talking can't see the whites of their eyes dark.

As service started the generator was cranked up and the keyboard soon plugged in. Min. Bill was asked to lead in worship. He played so hard that I still hear parts of the keyboard falling apart in the dark. As praise and worship ended in this pitch dark church made of only walls and dirt floors, no windows, doors or roof and make shift pews that were carried in by the children. Pastor Barber, our leader approached Min. Bill and says to him, I need you to minister...just like that. Bill was introduced to the interpreter and like a Porshe in the dark, he went from 0 to 60 in about 3 seconds! I quickly grabbed my Sony Cyber-Shot, turned on the flash and pointed it in the direction of the sound of his voice. Because of the flash the picture appears to be in a well lit area. When I reviewed the picture, this man was in full blown preaching. Arms flailing, voice booming, and Word flying...in the dark. This is my best description of On Demand. Min. Bill had no clue that he would be called on to minister in Word, but since he has been through The Lord's Chemo therapy, he fit the bill...no pun intended. He was free to minister in all capacities that the Lord presented him with.

When we go through the Lord's Chemo we may feel as if he is trying to drown us but take heart it is a simple cleansing from the master. Depending on our diagnosis, that determines what wash cycle we receive, delicates/knits, permanent press or 30 mins. Some of us are in a class by ourselves needing dry cleaning, which takes longer. Our needs also determines the amount of Water that He uses as well as the temperature of the Water.

Cleansing agents did not start off smelling as fabulous as they do today, because there sole purpose was to cleanse not to enjoy. We've all worn clothes with the idea of not getting it soiled in order to hang it up to wear again before cleaning, but that proved negative. Once the light was turned on the dirt was revealed. So it is with our lives, we have every intention of not getting dirty in order to be empowered to minister again without interruption. But once held up to the light(Word), the spots show up and The Master Doctor has to reach for the hyssop and administer until you and I are clean enough for Him to give us the Authority to Minister freely...On Demand.

Like me on today, are you willing to receive your Chemo from the Doctor!

Psalms 91:1-2

HE WHO dwells in the secret place of the Most High

shall remain stable and fixed under the shadow of the Almighty [Whose power no foe can withstand].

I will say of the Lord, He is my Refuge and my Fortress, my God; on Him I lean and rely, and in Him I [confidently] trust!

SIT, WALK, STAND

Before I started my treatments, some warriors that tread this path before me, informed me that my treatments would be accumulative. After each session, I along with my family would access my "feelings". In the beginning, I was sleeping more and eating less. I soon transferred to eating and sleeping. My daily showers required me to take a 2 hour nap.

After a short time, I was able to join Billy in his daily routine, which was walking. We enjoyed our late evening walks and talks. But around my fifth treatment, something happened. I had no strength or energy in my legs to walk anymore. Each time that I stood, I felt as if some invisible force was draining the energy from my hamstrings. I found myself holding on to doors, walls and people to get from point A to B. I prayed, I ate, I drank water, I slept, I rested, but nothing changed for a while.

If I was standing and you were talking to me, I understood nothing simply because all of my energy went into standing. I could look you in your eyes as you spoke to me but I felt like Charlie Brown listening to his teacher talk. Now, it's not so much the standing as it is the getting up.

In my mind, I went over my favorite biblical stories. The women with the issue of blood, the man laying and waiting for the angel to come trouble the waters, and the man that was born blind. As it was hard for me to stand, I had to lay... in my faith. As it pains me to get up, Praise God, I can now stand...in my faith.

I am comforted by knowing that wherever I find myself, Jesus is there, Psalms 139.

I was also humbled by the fact that He doesn't need me Ps. 50:12, but will use me if I submit myself to Him. And I am astounded by the truth that He loves me Jer. 31:3, and looks after me Ps. 8:4.

Wherever you are today, enjoy your walks and talks with Jesus and He can and will use you...right where you are.

Wanda Moultrie

HIS LOVE FOR ME

On June 6, 2016, my husband received an early call from my radiation doctor to have me at the hospital that morning in order to make the mask to be used for my treatment. We arrived all bright eyed and bushy tailed to see what God had in store for us. Bill and I had our consult, the mask was made and we were told to be back at 2:45 for my first round out of 10.

After our consult we ran a few errands and headed home. Being that we had a few hours before our appointment, Bill decided to drop me off at home while he went to get a bite to eat. In front of the house, I got out of his truck, walked around the backside, up on the curb, up the driveway and by the time I reached for my truck with my right hand, it was gone and I had a face full of dirt. I'd hit the ground like a tree that had been freshly cut. I lay there praying to God to get me into house. One thing I was sure of is that without Him, I could not move. He picked me up and as I look back on that day, the Spirit of God guided me into the house, because I lacked clarity.

Leslie helped me get cleaned up, and when Bill returned, I was setting at that table as if nothing happened, but I did make him aware of the fall.

Bill and I headed to the hospital for my new experience. At the hospital Bill parks his truck in says to me, don't move I will come get you. On our short walk across the parking lot, just outside the door my right knee buckled, then my left knee buckled. Before I could take another step, which felt very unstable, Bill had scooped me up purse and all and ran me to a safe place inside of the hospital. I was wearing a floor length sundress and flip flops. For once I felt safe and secure, he didn't stutter step, my dress didn't get caught in the two doors that he carried me through. He did not bump any part of my body. It was done so swiftly, without thinking...a premeditated action.

We being sheep, need a shepherd daily. Why, because we are dumb. If sheep are not sheered at the proper time and their wool grows continually, the sheep become "cast" meaning they fall over under the weight of their wool and cannot get up. They are then in need of a loving Shepherd to come and right them. In order to be "righted", the wool has to be sheered.

When my knees buckled it was the quick loving action of my husband that kept me from harm. He did not think about it, he did not draft up blueprints saying if she falls to the right then she will be in the parking lot and maybe under a car or if she falls to the left she will hit the beautiful water fountain. In his mind, in his heart, his love was in need and he did what true love does....it acts on behalf of the other.

Now you have to know that after 33 years of marriage

East Baltimore and West Philly have had quite a few disagreements, but the heart of this man showed, Song of Solomon 8:7 Many waters cannot quench love, neither can floods drown it.

Where did he learn this type of love from, you may ask your self. Having a relationship with our Savior has taught Bill well.

1 Peter 5:7 Casting the whole of your care [all your anxieties, all your worries, all your concerns, once and for all] on Him, for He cares for you affectionately and cares about you watchfull

As I was going along in my life, so I thought, I had become cast with wool or sin if you please. I could not right myself and the Savior, My Savior came along with His love and "righted" me through His death and resurrection.

If you have never been righted by the Savior, today is your day. No matter who thinks that you are a Christian but you really aren't, today is your day of salvation. You can freely go to God in prayer and empty out your heart. You do not need flowery words written by others, simply a sincere heart. He's lovingly waiting.

Romans 10:9-10

Because if you acknowledge and confess with your lips that Jesus is Lord and in your heart believe (adhere to, trust in, and rely on the truth) that God raised Him from the dead, you will be saved.

For with the heart a person believes (adheres to, trusts in, and relies on Christ) and so is justified (declared righteous, acceptable to God), and with the mouth he confesses (declares openly and speaks out freely his faith) and confirms [his] salvation.

STILL

We've heard this word all too many times. As children as someone dressed us, we were told to be still. When having our hair styled, we often heard the words, be still.

When working in conjunction with someone, we may have been told, hold this, but keep it still.

I remember as a child playing games...train, train, numba nine going down Chicago line. In order to play we had to put one foot in a circle and keep it still.

In school on picture day. just before the photographer took the picture we were told to sit still.

At the amusement park when we are about to be strapped in our ride, the attendant usually says, hands up and be still so that you can be strapped in.

In driving I was taught that if I was not certain I thatI could safely pass by another vehicle, that I should let the other vehicle proceed while I was still.

In lifting weights, the muscle being worked, for the most part has to be still in order to properly receive the execution.

For some of us that is hard to do, be still. Ok for me, it is hard to be still. I'm not a nervous ninny as my Mom used to call it, just moving to move, but I'm used to moving.

Grocery shopping, gardening, sewing, changing a light switch, cooking, driving a school bus, repairing a hot tub, all of these things require movement and I didn't mind moving.

Earlier in my salvation, the Lord gave me a female army friend named Tracey. We often shared in personal bible studies and fellowship for our growth, Our relationship was so close that the Holy Spirit would give her a verse for myself and because she worked for Uncle Sam, if she was not able to reach me for several days, God would then confirm that verse in my heart without having spoken with Tracey.

It was not a game, it was a testimony of our relationship with the Savior as well as one another.

The verse that sticks out in my mind in particular during this time in our relationship is Psalms 46:10, Be still and know that I am God.

At the time, I took it that God wanted me to stay planted in my parents home and not complain, be still right. So that's what I set my heart on doing.

This verse has to be a marathon runner, because it has pursued and tracked me down my entire life. After doing a Word study, years ago because of the tracking of this verse, I found that the word still means, without sound thought or movement. Now 2 out of 3 I can do. It's like trying to keep the 10 commandments. The more I work on the ones that I see, the more I become an offender of the others.

CAN YOU DRAW?

Growing up as a child in my house, there were four children. Joe, Faith, Chris and myself.

I don't know where my brother Joe obtained his drawing skills from as a child. None of his siblings had it, but like my mother used to say, he could draw like nobody's business.

In my family we are split. My husband is an excellent artist and he passed it on to Billy and Leslie. Stacey and Douglas are my kids when it comes to drawing. I always say in terms of myself that I can't draw a straight line with a ruler. Fear not, God has given us our talents as well. It is up to us whether or not we bury them or multiply them.

Myself, Stacey and Douglas are like some Christians when it comes to drawing. We tell ourselves that we can't do it. It's either the last thing on our list, or it's not on the list at all. Sometimes coxing or encouragement if you will from the right person will move us in that direction.

Concerning Christians we sometimes become comfortable with asking God to bless our food and watch over us when we sleep and thank you for getting me to church safely. God has to orchestrate occurrences in our lives in order to get His children to draw near to Him. We know that to be true because the Word declares that we only love Christ because He first loved us.

Ten or more years ago, I was on the highway yelling at my husband on the cell phone, when it sounded as if a truck was about to rear end me. I'm looking in all of my mirrors like a good bus driver does. And then it happened, I had my one and only (thank God) blow out. Well Bill was about 30 minutes behind me and let me tell you, I sat on the side of the highway praying for protection for myself and others in my position as well as his safe arrival like nobody's business. And wouldn't you know it he shows up like we weren't arguing.

He was concerned about me and my safety and getting my car up and running. Every since that day I have learned to pray earnestly for the protection and safety of others while traveling, near or far.

I have several grands whose noses will bleed seemingly because it wants to. One summer my grandson was here at our house and while he was in the bathtub acting as if he were floating on his back, his nose began to bleed so profusely that he began to choke and had to be rushed to the ER. Again, the Lord stretched my prayers for my grands as well as the grands of others.

Over the years and through these occurrences God has been teaching me how to draw. His promise to me is if I draw nigh to Him, that He will in turn draw nigh to me and then I can resist the devil and he will flee. God also promises that I can go boldly to the throne of Grace and receive MERCY, and find grace to help..

James 4:7-8

So be subject to God. Resist the devil [stand firm against him], and he will flee from you.

Come close to God and He will come close to you. [Recognize that you are] sinners, get your soiled hands clean; [realize that you have been disloyal] wavering individuals with divided interests, and purify your hearts [of your spiritual adultery].

Hebrews 4:16

Let us then fearlessly and confidently and boldly draw near to the throne of grace (the throne of God's unmerited favor to us sinners), that we may receive mercy [for our failures] and find grace to help in good time for every need [appropriate help and well-timed help, coming just when we need.

Is God teaching you how to draw and you can't seem to get the concept?

Philippians 1:6

And I am convinced and sure of this very thing, that He Who began a good work in you will continue until the day of Jesus Christ [right up to the time of His return], developing [that good work] and perfecting and bringing it to full completion in you.

https://youtu.be/JbEaftzaFWA

I Command

Most of us remember the song, I command. Well that's where I am today. A little over a month ago I was told by my radiation Doctor, following a fall that I had, that I have so much going on in my brain right now that the commands from my brain were getting slower. I was also told that there were constant fluctuations in my blood pressure that were going unnoticed by me, which resulted in my fall.

I had to be retaught how to get up and move from point a to point b. After taking so many daily meds, I basically turned into a sleeping, spaced out eating machine. I could literally feel the strength leaving my muscles as the pounds packed on.

It became a chore for me to shower everyday. On one particular day as the Lord woke me up, the words to the afore mentioned song flooded my heart. I told my husband that I wanted to go for a walk. He loaded my walker with the seat and wheels and we headed out. He cautioned me not to over do it and he stayed close by my side. Before I made a move I had to tell my brain (like Dr. Suess), left foot, right foot, left foot, right.

At the attendance of Minister Moultrie's Ordination Service, I literally had to command my eyes to focus on faces, remember who they are, have a conversation, breathe, not go to sleep as I had been accustomed to for the past month.

First I had to put in a request to my Abba Father, that I needed to walk upstairs, that I needed His strength, ability, and His intellect. After all He said to ask and ye shall receive.

The next day I found myself doing the same, saying you need to walk up the stairs, while holding your cup of tea and your water bottle, without dropping them...and I made it.

Now for the question, where would we all be if everyday, every second we would do this with Christ. I command my mouth to speak what is edifying to the hearer. Ephesians 4:29

Let no foul or polluting language, nor evil word nor unwholesome or worthless talk [ever] come out of your mouth, but only such [speech] as is good and beneficial to the spiritual progress of others, as is fitting to the need and the occasion, that it may be a blessing and give grace (God's favor) to those who hear it. I command my heart to pray and meditate on Gods Word. Joshua 1:8

This Book of the Law shall not depart out of your mouth, but you shall meditate on it day and night, that you may observe and do according to all that is written in it. For then you shall make your way prosperous, and then you shall deal wisely and have good success. Psalms 1:2

But his delight and desire are in the law of the Lord, and on His law (the precepts, the instructions, the teachings of

God) he habitually meditates (ponders and studies) by day and by night. I command my life to please the Lord.

Romans 12

I APPEAL to you therefore, brethren, and beg of you in view of [all] the mercies of God, to make a decisive dedication of your bodies [presenting all your members and faculties] as a living sacrifice, holy (devoted, consecrated) and well pleasing to God, which is your reasonable (rational, intelligent) service and spiritual worship.

Live a lifestyle consistent with Gods Word and purposely go out and share the Good News of Christ.

Ephesians 6:15

And having shod your feet in preparation [to face the enemy with thefirm-footed stability, the promptness, and the readiness produced by the good news] of the Gospel of peace.

Matthew 28:19

Go then and make disciples of all the nations, baptizing them into the name of the Father and of the Son and of the Holy Spirit,

Psalms 63:4

So will I bless You while I live; I will lift up my hands in Your name.

Psalms 119:48

My hands also will I lift up [in fervent supplication] to Your commandments, which I love, and I will meditate on Your statutes.

All together now MOUTH PRAISE THE LORD, HEART PRAISE THE LORD, LIFE PRAISE THE LORD, HEART PRAISE THE LORD.

FALLOW GROUND

Singing in my Marvin Winan's voice, Break up that Fallow Ground. If you are under 40, you may not be familiar with this song, but you can find it on YouTube.

This was and still is one of my favorite songs. I remember hearing sermons about breaking up fallow ground. Fallow ground was usually referred to as a stony heart that had not been plowed.

After becoming a Berean, I found that fallow ground is ground that has been dug up for planting, but the planting has never taken place. The ground has been left unattended in that position for about 2-3 years. This state is actually worse than the first. Before the ground was touched it was better off. It was at least level ground, all in need of the same thing. Once dug up for planting and left in that position, you have ditches and hills, clumps and lumps and once the rain and sun beats down upon it, it sort of freezes or forms in that state. In order to plant, instead of working with level ground, your work is much harder because of the unevenness, unsteadiness of the ground. The ground was dug up for a purpose that it never received.

So it is with our hearts. When God dug up our hearts to give us a heart of flesh and we refused to plant the Word in its place it left a complete rocky, clumpy uneven mass of flesh!

Sow for yourselves according to righteousness (uprightness and right standing with God); reap according to mercy and loving-kindness. Break up your uncultivated ground, for it is time to seek the Lord, to inquire for and of Him, and to require His favor, till He comes and teaches you righteousness and rains His righteous gift of salvation upon you (Hosea 10:12).

Remember the parable of the sower and the seed in Matt. 13:4...the seed needs to fall on "good" ground to take root and bring forth some 30, 60 and 100 fold.

In gardening you cannot plant year after year in the same spot without amending or fixing the soil. The plants will grow weaker, not producing as much and eventually be non existent.

The key to amending the soil first is knowing what the problem is. An improper diagnosis has never corrected the flesh and surely not the heart!

BREAK UP THAT FALLOW GROUND.

Sent from my iPad

All bible references within this manuscript have been taken from the Amplified version of the bible.

Printed in the United States
By Bookmasters